# REAL ESTATE
## MY LIFE STORY

*A must-read for all real estate professionals.*

## MAC CHAMPSEE

First printing
This is a work of fiction. Any similarity between the characters and situations within its pages and places or persons, living or dead, is unintentional and coincidental.

Real Estate—My Life Story: A must-read for all real estate professionals is printed in Cambria.

Credits: Cover font: Times New Roman.
Cover art: "Real Estate Buildings Logo with buildings, houses, and tree silhouette" | Twindesigner | Depositphotos.com.

# Table of Contents

1. Modest Beginnings...............................................................5

2. Coming to Canada ..............................................................16

3. Disaster in Canada—My First Setback.............................25

4. Rainbow Realty—Ups and Downs....................................34

5. Lawsuits and more Lawsuits .............................................44

6. Pharmaceutical Manufacturing.........................................49

7. Lessons Learned.................................................................55

8. Why Real Estate?...............................................................58

9. Knowledge is Power and Experiene is a Valuable Asset...........61

10. Work is Never Wasted .....................................................64

11. How Experts Complicate Simple Criteria.......................69

12. You don't need to be "Smart" to Make Money ..............72

13. Experience is Useful, but Vision is the Key....................75

14. Perfect Bargains do not Exist..........................................77

15. Some Interesting Situations.............................................79

16. Real Estate is about Adding Value..................................82

17. Any Time is a Good Time to Buy ....................................86

18. Don't Read the News—Read the Classifieds .................88

19. Too Busy Making a Living................................................91

20. Learn how to Borrow .......................................................93

21. Invest in your own Backyard ...........................................96

22. Sales Seminars..................................................................98

23. Are All Tenants Problems? ............................................100

24. Categories of Real Estate .................................................. 102

25. Investment Analysis ........................................................ 106

26. Special-purpose Housing ................................................. 110

27. Real Estate vs. the Stock Market .................................... 113

28. Condo Conversions ......................................................... 116

29. Syndications and Joint Ventures .................................... 120

30. Believe in your Product .................................................. 122

31. The Importance of Trust ................................................ 124

# MODEST BEGINNINGS

We are originally from the northwest of India, and our province borders with Pakistan. It is mostly a desert area, and the rainfall is scanty and uncertain. Some years, it does not rain at all. The province we come from is known as Kutch Pradesh, which is now a part of Gujarat in India. A few hundred years back, our family migrated from Rajasthan to Kutch, which is also an arid region, and settled in a small village called Undoth, which had no running water, no electricity, and no toilet or shower facilities until the 1980s. Kutch was more promising than Rajasthan at the time. It was believed the soil in the area around Undoth was more fertile than the place from which the family had come.

As a child, I was lucky to have known my great-grandfather. His first name was Deraj, and he was Jesang Rambhiya's son. Some of us still bear his surname. [1] He was a farmer. Later in his life, he ventured to Bombay (now

---

[1] When I got to Canada, I dropped the name Rambhiya as it was difficult for others to spell and pronounce. Instead, I made my middle name, Champsee (which is also my father's first name), my surname. Since my arrival, I have been known as Mac Champsee because the name, Mac, is familiar locally and easier to say/deal with than my original first name, Motilal.

known as Mumbai) in a small boat in the late 1800s. It took them about two weeks to reach Mumbai during which they survived mainly on carrots and radishes. My great-grandfather started off selling homemade sweets in Mumbai to make some money, but he did not like it very much, and he went back to Undoth.

My grandfather—Deraj's son, Versee—was also a farmer. He had some schooling and was good at accounting. In the late 1920s, he got a job with a well-established Kutchi firm in Colombo that took him to Colombo, Ceylon (now known as Sri Lanka). He stayed there for a few years and visited his hometown from time to time. My father and his brothers had the opportunity to live in Colombo, and his two younger brothers studied there, as well.

In the 1930s, his employer offered my grandfather a small share in the company as an incentive. In 1932, he received the sum of 32,000 rupees, which was a fortune for him. He decided to retire, as it was far too much money for him to spend, and he went back to Undoth and built a nice bungalow. He also decided to return to farming while in Undoth.

Versee was an honest, well-respected man. It is said that he was very religious and that he helped many people in the village. One demonstration of his generosity is that as the fields were filled with valuable crops, it was necessary for Versee to sleep at the farm to guard it against thieves. He reached the farm one evening as it was getting dark, and he saw, at some distance, a man who had bundled a large supply of Versee's harvested grain in a piece of cloth. The man was trying to lift the bundle, but it was very heavy. He saw my grandfather coming, and because he did not recognize him, he hailed him and asked him to give him a hand so that he could put the bundle on his head to carry it to his home. My grandfather gave him a hand, knowing full well that he was stealing his crop, but he called him by his name and told him to take it this time but not to do such a thing ever again. Such was the generosity of this man.

My grandfather had four children with my grandmother, Purbai: my father, Champsee, the eldest, was born in 1903, Kanji was second, and Lalji was third. The fourth child was a girl. Both Kanji and Lalji were with my grandfather for a few years in Colombo. Lalji completed his Cambridge studies and was fluent in English. Champsee also learned English after he got to Burma, but he was not very fluent.

While my grandfather was working in Colombo, his employers told him they needed someone for their office in Rangoon, Burma, and they asked him to recommend one of his sons. Versee decided Champsee should take the position. He was only around fourteen at the time, but he was quite mature and willing to go and learn.

The company had about eleven rice mills in Burma that would remove the husk—which was used for fuel—and then ship rice to Rangoon. In those years, Burma was a major exporter of rice to many countries. Champsee proved to be brilliant, and after a few years, he was promoted to the position of manager.

Champsee had a real business acumen and was good at decision making. One year, there was a shortage of rice, and it was a challenge to get the required quantities to keep the mills running. Champsee started offering slightly higher prices and got commitments from suppliers for quantities needed for export. Some of his colleagues were puzzled, and they did not like the fact Champsee was offering higher prices. They complained to the boss, who called Champsee into his office. Champsee explained that eleven rice mills had to be fed every day and that if he waited to strike a bargain, the sale price was bound to go up anyway. In that case, it was possible the company would end up paying a much higher price. By getting a commitment, he was assured of the quantities needed. Of course, the boss understood the situation, and he thanked Champsee for his decision in the matter.

Champsee settled in Burma, and he called my mother, Rajbai, to join him in the early 1930s. My eldest sister was born in Burma. At that time, the family lived in residential quarters adjoining one of the rice mills. Rajbai was pretty good at managing things at home, and she carried on with the farming in Kutch, going back and forth to Burma every now and then.

Japan attacked Burma in the early 1940s, and many people, like my father, decided to return to India to avoid being bombed by the Japanese Air Force. I was born in Undoth in 1942.

Champsee lived in Bombay for a number of years during the Japanese occupation after he returned from Burma, but he never quite settled there. One of his brothers, Kanji, was carrying on with the spice business in Bombay, and the youngest, Lalji, had settled in Colombo.

In or about 1945, when the Japanese left Burma, Bogyoke Aung San fought for Burma's independence from Britain, a goal that was achieved on the fourth of January, 1948. Soon after that, many people from India, who had lived earlier in Burma, started to go back.

My father returned to Burma in 1946, deciding to move the family back to Rangoon in 1950. I was barely eight years of age when I started school in Rangoon.

In Burma, my father was active as a produce broker. He got my elder brother, Morarji, to join him, and together, they made a reasonable living. My father asked Kanji if he wanted to come to Burma, and he got his family to settle there. Champsee helped many other people get settled in Burma. It is said that someone wanted to come to Rangoon on one occasion, but he could not get the necessary passport. My father found a friend who had a passport but did not want to return to Burma. He asked the friend to give the man his passport, as it was of no use to him. He replaced his friend's photograph with that of the person who wanted to settle in Burma. The idea worked, and this other fellow was able to settle in Rangoon and earn a reasonable living.

Looking back, I can see that Champsee and his two brothers were ahead of their time. They were the first to venture out from the village of Undoth. My grandmother married off all three brothers as arranged marriages were the norm in those days. In my opinion, all three brothers were married to the wrong women. My mother knew how to read and write a little, but the other women were completely illiterate. If all of the brothers had been able to choose their life partners, they would have been better off, however, that was not the way it was done in those days.

It was my father's desire to see me well-educated. Although he had worked for a company for a few years, he was firmly against me working for anyone else. He would say that once one is in the habit of working for someone else, one loses the desire to be an entrepreneur. These words were an inspiration to me.

In my final years of schooling, many people from my class wanted to go into engineering. None of us studying in Burma could gain admission to its universities as we'd only been educated in English and Gujarati, our native language. As a result, we had to find a college in India offering engineering courses in English or Gujarati. However, my father was never in favour of going back to India, and he certainly did not want to send me there, because he was not in favour of me becoming an engineer and go to work for someone else. I had a big argument with him, and he said that he would not support me if I decided to go to India. He told me that if I became an independent businessman, I could employ engineers to work for me. As a result, I went to Tagore College in Rangoon which had an affiliation with Calcutta University and which offered us art classes. In the later years, I tutored some students and made some money. My father was furious when he found out and asked me to stop immediately. He was concerned that once I had worked for others, I would get into that habit and never become a businessman on my own. I somehow convinced him to allow me to carry on with the tutoring, as it was only temporary.

My father did reasonably well in his business as an export broker, but he did not send money to India as he never believed that he or any other members of the family would ever go back. Things in Burma were changing, however, and they changed for the worst.

It so happened that Prime Minister U Nu—a contemporary of Mahatma Gandhi and Jawaharlal Nehru of India—had difficulties with some communities in Burma in the late 1950s. At one point in the early 1960s, U Nu willingly handed the reins of power to General Ne Win, Chief of the Burmese Army. The army did an awesome job of restoring peace and harmony, however, they got a taste of power in the process.

The army seized power in a coup in the latter part of 1962. They jailed all the cabinet ministers—thirty-two of them—in one night. The following morning, they declared that they had taken power for the good of the country. Many of us did not take this seriously, since the army had done a fine job of administering the country for the nine months after U Nu had handed over the power, however, it is believed the Chinese influenced the army chiefs, and the army started nationalizing all the businesses, banks and schools. My friend Samir worked for the Hong Kong and Shanghai Bank, which became the People's Bank No. 9 when it was nationalized. Similarly, all the stores simply became People's stores. Army generals and colonels managed everything, but they did not know a thing about business, which created much chaos.

The army did several other things. They required one person from every household to clean the streets with once a week with a broom. We were also required to guard the streets one night a month. Businesses suffered greatly because of the government takeover. Many of us started dealing in cash rather than banking it.

One day, the government announced that all currency notes over the sum of fifty kyats would no longer be legal tender. Anyone who had cash was required to report it to government officials. If they reported large amounts, they were questioned as to how they got the money. As a result, many people with large cash reserves sold currency notes for a nominal sum to those who didn't have much to declare. Bank accounts were frozen, and people needed to get permission from army personnel in charge of bank management if they needed to withdraw large sums of money. Permission was not easy to get.

My father had a great shock when he lost his livelihood, leaving him with no means of supporting his family. I was a student at the time, and I tried to help him. Burmese nationals worked for low wages for the government as we were not allowed to engage in private enterprises because we were Indian citizens.

One incident I remember is about a business associate of my father's, to whom he owed a commission. My father told him that he could not pay since he had not received the commission from which he was to pay the man his share. This failure of payment resulted in the business associate consulting a lawyer to get a stay order from the court, preventing my father from leaving Burma without paying him. Somebody overheard the conversation in that lawyer's office and informed my elder brother and me that a stay order for my father was in process which would prohibit him from leaving Burma. My brother said there was not much we could do about it. I, however, had an idea and went straight to the Rangoon High Court to search out this lawyer. Since we did not know each other, I told him that I had been sent by his client to give him the message that Champsee had settled everything and it was no longer necessary to pursue the stay order. The lawyer took my words at face value and told me to tell his client that the case would be withdrawn, but he would be responsible for the stamp duty and some out-of-pocket expenses.

I then made arrangements for my father to leave for India the very next morning, making sure he reached the airport in time. The next day, of course, his client came to know the actual situation and shouted at me. I told him that I was just a student and had no money to give him and that he could do whatever he wanted about it, but the matter ended there.

I was a bright student, scoring first in the final examinations. My strengths were English and grammar. We had an excellent teacher who knew Greek and Latin as well as English, however, a couple of teachers made grammatical errors in the notes they gave us. One day, I decided to go through their errors, and I wrote a letter addressed to the principal, thinking she would praise me for being a bright student. A friend of mine, Niranjan, read the letter and asked if I would include his name on it. We handed the letter over, and after a couple of hours, you could see the anger on the principal's face. The letter was read in front of the entire class. She suggested that we were black sheep and should be dismissed. Although the administration did not take those steps, Niranjan and I decided to leave the school of our own to attend another one.

I am quite resourceful, and even as a student, I prepared notes that I duplicated on the school's Gestetner machine.

Geography was my favourite subject, and I prepared notes for others in that subject and in English to facilitate their studies. The notes were useful guides for many students, and they helped them in their final exams. I also made some money in the process.

Another incident concerned a famous Indian actor who came to Rangoon about 1961. I was able to obtain only one ticket to the performance, but since my friend, Bipin, was also eager to go, I quickly came up with an idea. We were in a small shop, and I asked the shopkeeper to give me a pair of scissors and some cardboard. I cut the cardboard the same size as the invitation card and put that inside the envelope that came with the invitation. We glued it closed and went to the gate at the venue where the performance was to be held. One of us handed over the original, sealed envelope with the cardboard inside, and the other, the original invitation card, and we were both admitted and thoroughly enjoyed the event.

As the political and living situations were getting out of hand in Burma and many Indians went back to India, we realized we also might have to leave soon, so my friend and I thought we should visit some places of interest before we left. We went by foot to Kyaithiyo, on which there is a golden pagoda, on a large stone, sitting precariously on the edge of a cliff. There was a Buddhist festival where there were hundreds of pilgrims. We saw that a large tent had been put up and that most of the people had found a place to sleep inside the tent. It was quite hot and muggy inside, and we thought it best to sleep outside in the open.

A couple of hours later, the weather turned freezing cold, so we put on all of the shirts we had and buried our heads in whatever we had to protect us from the cold. We would never forget that experience.

Thingyan is a Burmese water festival marking the start of a new season in which people gather in throngs and drive around in open lorries while others throw water on them as a sign of welcome. A friend and I decided to go to Moulmein with other people who went by train. The train was fully packed, and we only had standing room. We did not have much luggage and had brought nothing to eat, thinking we would buy something to eat along the way. Unfortunately, the stations sold hardly anything for us to eat as we were both vegetarians, and we both starved as a result. Many of the other passengers had, however, brought things to eat, and most of that food was stored on the upper shelves of the train in tiffin carriers or boxes. Kirit and I would gently open the containers to help ourselves to a few sweets and other edibles. We would get off at the next station, eat the food, get back on the train, and move to the next compartment. We somehow fed ourselves this way until we reached Moulmein, where we ate well.

I also did some travelling with Bipin, my close friend, who had gone to India to take up engineering studies. When he visited us in Burma in 1964, he and I decided to go on a tour of the country. We were on a shoestring budget, but we had great fun.

My father left Burma in early 1964, and the rest of the family—my elder brother and his family and my mother— left a couple of months later. I was to wind up the household, complete my third year in the B.A. program at Tagore College and then leave. We all knew that going to India and settling there would be tough as the opportunities there were limited when compared to those in Burma. This is why another friend and I thought to go somewhere abroad. Rangoon was the capital of Burma. It was where all of the foreign embassies were located, and so we were able to apply for visas to England, Australia, Germany, Italy, Switzerland, and the U.S.A. Unfortunately, each of these places was difficult to get into, and there was a long waiting period.

One day, I came across a copy of the *Canada Year Book 1964* at the British Council Library. In it, I learned that about a quarter of a million immigrants settled in Canada every year. They got government assistance and were finding jobs. It was a step in the right direction. Canada did not have an embassy in Rangoon, but we found out that the British Embassy handled everything for Canada.

We got the application forms for permanent residence from the British Embassy and were interviewed by a Canadian high commissioner who visited Rangoon every few months from the New Delhi High Commission. In our interview, we were advised to get letters of interest from Canadian firms and resubmit the applications. We received some letters of interest from a few firms, our applications were eventually approved, and we landed in Canada.

# 2
# COMING TO CANADA

It was August of 1964 we still had not received our visas. Nevertheless, we decided to leave for India. After arriving in India, we visited the Canadian High Commission in New Delhi to pursue our case. We struggled to obtain the necessary visas, which finally arrived in the spring of 1965.

Samir had cousins in Calcutta, and they invited us to live with them. We shared a room with eight of them, but the room only had one bathroom, so it was always a challenge to get going in the morning. Samir was able to find a job with a bank since he had already worked in one for a few years in Rangoon. I had some experience in my father's business. I also had very good skills in typing and shorthand.

Getting jobs in India was not easy in those days. I started by looking at the ads in the newspapers. The first one I saw in the *Hindustan Standard* was for a typist, and I applied for it. I did not expect to even get an interview, however, I got a call and immediately landed a job with pay that was about $1.25 per day, which what one could expect then.

The company I worked dealt in pipe fittings and plumbing supplies. They were wholesalers who supplied their goods to many parts of India. Every day, they would receive twenty to thirty letters for enquiries or quotes, and my job was to sit with the boss, get instructions, and type up replies. I would also enclose price lists and other information if they were necessary.

After the first few days, I asked my boss why he had selected me for the job when there had been about ninety applicants, most of whom were more qualified than I. My boss told me that I would find my answer once I looked at the file containing the applications. I looked through the file, and I kept coming back to my application because it was the only one that stood out. It was well-typed, on a good quality paper, with proper formatting. So, that was the answer for which I was looking. From very early on, I had the habit of trying my best and always put my best foot forward. I do not spare any effort in any task I am given. This is a quality that helped me tremendously later on in my working life.

As for our B.A. studies, Samir and I had to appear for our final examination at Calcutta University. Attending the classes to study was not mandatory; one could study at home. Given our limited time, we took advantage of this option, appeared for the final examination in May 1965, and managed to get through it successfully, made possible by the college in Rangoon being affiliated with the University of Calcutta.

Since there was not much information available about Canada in those days, we were unaware of its lifestyle, job availability, and how new immigrants settled there. Hence, we were uncertain about our ability to settle in Canada in the future. If nothing worked, we were prepared to return to India.

It was difficult to leave the family, and my mother was not willing to let me go. My father, however, was happy to see me go to Canada as he did not believe I would find suitable work in India, which meant earning enough to support my parents as well my brother and his four kids.

While still in India, I started to look for pen pals from Canada since we knew no one there, nor did we know where to go once we would arrive. In those days, some magazines carried names, addresses, and interests of individuals in different parts of the world who wanted to develop friendships with others from other parts of the world. (There was no email or Internet in those days.) I wrote to some people in Canada and received replies from three, one in Vancouver, another in Nova Scotia, and a third in Montreal. Based on my pen pal's advice we settled on Montreal, Canada since that was where she lived.

We began to plan our journey to Canada, based on a budget we could afford. I was able to borrow some funds from Niranjan Kamdar's father. (Niranjan had been in my class back in my school days.)

In those days, India had very tight foreign exchange controls. A traveler was allowed to take only eight dollars with him for an overseas trip. We somehow managed to bring around $50, and we started out from Bombay on the *Gugliemo Marconi*, a ship operated by Lloyd Treistino. We were able to visit Aden and see the pyramids in Egypt while the ship crossed from Alexandria to Port Said. The side trips we took were not very expensive.

There were six of us in the cabin. We made friends with the other occupants and were able to borrow $50 from one of them.

With hardly any cash, we landed in Genoa about a week later. After touring the city, we took the train to Zurich where we spent the night at the Swiss Air office, giving the staff the excuse that we had to catch an early morning flight.

Next, we went to Paris, where we put ourselves up at the railway station in the evening. As bad luck would have it, we were asked to move around midnight as the railway station was closing for the night. We somehow passed the night at a streetcar stop.

After that, we took the train to Stuttgart, where we had a connection to catch. There was one known individual who put us up at a bed and breakfast place, and we stayed for a couple of days there.

By the time we took the train and boat via Dover to Victoria Terminus in London, England, we had no money left. I did, however, have a friend in UK—Samir—and we were able to spend the next three or four days in London with him. Samir was able to borrow about $500 from a friend of his who was an Oxford professor. This was the only capital we had when we landed in Montreal, Canada to help us settle there.

My pen pal had made reservations for us at the local YMCA. We stayed there for almost a week but had no luck finding a job, mainly because we did not speak French. One day, the secretary at the YMCA called us and said, "Boys, what are you doing in Montreal?"

We told him we were looking for jobs.

He said, "You are looking for jobs in the wrong place. Take the train to Toronto." By then, we were down to $275 of the $500 loan, so we took the train to Toronto.

We arrived in Toronto around middle of July 1965 and stayed in an old downtown hotel for a couple of days. Someone in Montreal had given us the name of an Indian gentleman with an importing business who was among the early Sikh settlers in Toronto. He used to wear a turban and beard, but due to his surroundings, he had shaved the beard and gotten rid of the turban.

When we went to see him, he gave us some sound, practical advice, and we had our first good Indian dinner, prepared by his wife. Because Samir wore a beard in those days, the gentleman asked, "Why are you keeping a beard? You are better off not having it."

Samir took his advice and shaved off his beard. We also came to know that the man had some real estate holdings in Toronto and the surrounding area.

The next noteworthy thing that happened after we arrived in Toronto was meeting Herb Mackenzie while we searched for accommodations. We moved into one of the rooms he rented at 59 Walmer Road in Toronto's Annex area and started our lives in the city. Herb was also instrumental in starting my career in real estate, which I talk about in later chapters of this book.

When we landed in Toronto, my only skill had been typing. I came across a temporary employment agency by the name of Office Overload and went for an interview. They determined that, although I was overqualified, given my B.A., I had excellent typing skills. (I was able to do about eighty words a minute.) They said that although that type of work was normally done by the girls there, they didn't mind trying me out as I seemed to have a good command of typing, and I did it without making any errors.

As a result, I was employed on the fourth or fifth day after my arrival in Toronto. The pay was $1.50 per hour, which, in those days, was great for me. I was able to pay all of the expenses for both of us with the money. I carried on with my work for Office Overload for the next few months while I looked for a better job.

While we were searching for jobs, I had a couple of funny experiences with *The Toronto Star*, which was filled with classified ads for employment. In those days, the newspaper was the best medium with which to advertise as there were no computers and no Internet. One day, I saw an ad with the heading, "Indian Affairs Branch". I said to my friend, "Look—they happen to have a special branch for us, coming from India." When I phoned them, I discovered I was the wrong kind of Indian—the branch was meant for Canadian aboriginals.

There was another ad with the heading "HANDICAPPED? We Can Help". I called them, and the person on the other end asked, "What kind of handicap do you have?" I told him that our handicap was that we could not find jobs. The person laughed and explained to me that they helped people with physical handicaps or disabilities. It was a while before we were used to Canadian English.

One day, I read an ad about a job opening at the Magistrates' Court Office at Old City Hall. They needed a cashier, and so I went there and had an interview with the supervisor. Each day, the employee was to take in cash or cheques for parking violations and summonses, followed by some bookkeeping. I was quite capable of doing that, however, when the supervisor learned that I had a Bachelor of Arts degree, he thought I would leave as soon as I got something better. For that reason, he was not keen to offer me the position.

I refused to give up. I also told him about my typing skills—I know he could sense from my pronunciation and manners that I was new to the country—he told me they were looking for a non-typist. I said I had no problem becoming a non-typist—all I had to do was not to type. He then told me they needed someone to do the photocopying. I think he knew that coming from a country like India, I probably did not know what a photocopier looked like—he was right.

He took me to the Xerox machine, gave me a page, and asked me to copy it, but I couldn't figure out how to go about it. I told him that the copying machine with which I was familiar was a fair bit different, that it was like taking a photograph and developing it—which was a hobby of mine. He started to laugh. Then, he took the page from me, put it face down on the screen, pressed a switch, and out came the crisp copy.

He said, "Well, this is how you copy here," and hired me anyway at $2.25 per hour, which was much better than what I was making as a typist.

It was my perseverance that got me the job. I bring that trait to almost everything I do because I have always believed that persistence pays. This is one characteristic that has handsomely rewarded me all of my life.

I started working at the Magistrates Court Office and became quite friendly with other employees. As my first name was Motilal, they started calling me Mo, which I didn't care for as it meant "like dead" in my mother tongue. This is why I told them to call me Mac. To this day, I am still known as Mac Champsee.

Although my friend and I had had no idea what we might do in Canada, we now seemed to be getting somewhere. He had a job at the University of Toronto Libraries, which suited him fine.

I was always interested in a career in accounting. While we were in Burma, my father frequently insisted that a good knowledge of accounts was essential for any business. Because I did not want to make a career out of my job at the Magistrates Office, I kept my eyes and ears open for other opportunities, which is how I came across an ad in *The Toronto Star* for an articled clerk in a chartered accountant's office. I called them for an interview and got an appointment to see somebody at his firm, located at the corner of Yonge and King.

It was a fairly lengthy interview. I was the first East Indian he had ever met, and he was more curious than anything else. I was fairly good at English except for my pronunciation. He told me that he had six other partners and that he would need to consult some of them before he got back to me.

I called him after a couple of days and was told that although he had quite liked me, he could not offer me the job as I did not have much Canadian experience and his partners were not sure about hiring me. I told him that the least he could do was to arrange interviews with his partners. I also told him that I did not mind seeing all of them. Again, I did not want to take no for an answer, and I wanted to leave no stone unturned.

He simply could not refuse my request, and he arranged for me to see one of his senior partners, which seemed to go well. When he asked me what I thought about the Canadian people, I had to tell him that Canadians were good people except that they did not want to take a chance with someone who did not have Canadian experience. He arranged for me to see another partner, whom I found to be very good.

I ended up getting the job at the firm at an initial salary of $60 per week. I also took accounting and auditing courses through the Institute of Chartered Accountants of Ontario.

Life at the firm was pretty good, and I learned a lot. I had a senior under whom I had to work. We would go to various clients and do their accounting or auditing. I started getting raises as I graduated from courses offered by the Institute of Chartered Accountants.

Samir and I started a business under the name of Torontrade, and started offering foreign exchange services to my contacts who wanted to send money to India. Most Indian immigrants who had to support their families in India came to us instead of the banks as offered better rates and services. We were able to offer better rates than banks since we were working with lower profit margins. Although the total volume wasn't great, it did give us some extra income which was a big help.

Next, we started importing handicrafts from India not commonly available in those days. My elder brother in India selected the goods and arranged to ship them to us in Canada. We would then go to gift shops in Toronto to sell the articles. The profit margin was good, but the volume was limited as we did not have much capital with which to work. Also, the business was part-time. Nonetheless, we learned a lot. We also started importing goods from Korea, Japan, and other places.

In 1968, I decided to go to India and find contacts for importing gift articles along the way. I also wanted to try to get married if I was able to find the right life partner in India. In the meantime, my friend would look after everything we were doing in Toronto. I gave him total power of attorney, took three months' unpaid leave from my job, and off I went.

I visited Japan, Korea, Hong Kong, and Burma before landing in India. Things took longer in India, and I ended up staying there for over six months. Although arranged marriages were still in style in those days, the usual practice was for the girls and boys to meet once or twice before deciding.

I was married on the seventh of November, 1968, and left for Canada after about two weeks since my return to work at the accounting firm was overdue, and it would take few months for my wife to get her necessary documents.

# DISASTER IN CANADA—MY FIRST SETBACK

I got back to Toronto sometime in the middle of November 1968, after almost seven months' absence. As soon as I entered the home on Kendal Avenue, I was taken aback, and suddenly very nervous. Everywhere I looked, I saw nothing but merchandise from all over the world. The basement, which had been almost empty when I had left, was now full of goods. While I was away, Samir had imported stuff from everywhere.

To meet the financial requirements, he borrowed against the house, getting about $5,000 at sixteen percent interest—a figure unheard of in those days. He insisted that I was very slow in everything and that he had to get the goods so that he could take part in the upcoming annual gift show at the Canadian National Exhibition. He ordered most of the merchandise shipped by air, which added quite a lot to the cost. I could see what was coming next: I visualized financial disaster.

To add insult to injury, Samir had taken money from clients who wanted us to transfer funds for them to India. He kept delaying payment to their family members in India, using the money to pay for the imports instead. The delay resulted in one arranged marriage being cancelled due to the funds not reaching them in time. Consequently, word had gone around in the community that we were delaying remittances and using the funds for personal use. It was not Samir's intention to cheat anyone, but his actions hurt us badly.

I had no idea what my partner was doing while I was away. He never mentioned a word about all of the purchases he made in my absence. I do not panic easily, and I always think of solutions rather than problems, but this large amount of inventory was bound to ruin us financially. I had heated arguments with him many times but to no avail, as he kept arguing that we needed all of the goods to build our business. I just could not convince him that he was totally wrong and that his decisions were really going to hurt us.

Given the circumstances, I had to make one of the toughest decisions of my life. I could not carry on with Samir because it would tarnish my name in the community, and that's why I decided to get out of the business. After some months of discussion, I had to take over some loans, give up my share in the house, and move out as a part of the settlement. I had my C.A. studies to complete, besides. However, I did learn a lesson that I will never forget, and I could see the importance of a good agreement, one that spells everything out. Samir and I did not have any such agreement because everything was based on trust.

In the meantime, another friend of mine, Ramesh Mody, had come to Toronto. He was originally from Burma but was able to get to England. He had some money, and he told me that he would support me temporarily, if necessary.

Also, the paperwork for my wife, Lata, was just about complete. She arrived in Toronto by air in August 1969. While in India, I had told her that I was doing well in Canada and was the co-owner of a large house. However, there I was in a situation in which I had nothing left to my name. On top of everything else, had loans to pay.

In fact, my situation was worse than when I had first started in Canada. In the beginning, I had nothing, but I did not have liabilities either. Now, I did. I had a tough time explaining everything to my wife. She had, however, come from a business family and had seen her father's ups and downs, and she understood and did not panic. Instead, she lent me support as I started out all over again.

Because my income was not sufficient to meet our expenses after my wife joined me, I had to borrow money from my friend, Ramesh, every month. I rented a one-bedroom apartment on Keele Street near High Park and started my life all over again.

Soon after Lata's arrival, I took her to the lawyer who had been retained by my ex-partner as my wife had to give up her dower rights when I gave up my interest in the house. You can imagine the scene: she had come to Toronto with high hopes, and I had to get her to sign off her dower rights on whatever I owned, plus take on a bank loan of $2000.

This was how our lives together began, but we did not give up hope. All of the people who used to send money home through us found out that it was not I who had been the culprit but my partner, and they all came back to me to persuade me to start the business again. I did so with my friend Ramesh, under the name of Pacific Traders, as he was living on a street by that name. The company did reasonably well.

Next, I formed another enterprise, called Overseas Trade Company, and started to import handicrafts from India and selling them to the contacts we had made earlier on. I did not have a retail outlet, and therefore, all goods were sold wholesale to various gift shops and stores. The business also provided an additional income. One of the items that was lightweight and good for a mail-order business was a hundred elephants on a bean, which I will write more on later. My wife also had a job with Office Overload. After working for a few months, she was able to get a job with Canada Life.

In addition to my regular income, I started earning some additional income from time to time with referrals from a real estate salesman, about whom I write in chapters following. I continued with my studies and was able to graduate as a chartered accountant in 1971. I had the opportunity to work with some of the clients from our firm who were real estate developers, and I learned even more about this line of business. I could see the opportunities that real estate would offer in the time to come.

One such client was in Oakville. He used to talk to me about the interesting deals he had made, and his stories gave me more insight into what could be done in the future. One day, he told me his partner had attended a real estate auction in Oakville and bought a 100-acre farm for $32,000. When the zoning was changed from agricultural to residential, the property was resold for $1,000,000—a tremendous amount of money in those days. On top of that, in 1971, when this sale took place, there was no capital gains tax in Canada.

I could see that real estate was a highly lucrative business.

After graduating as a chartered accountant, I worked for the same accounting firm for another year or so and then left the firm to join a real estate firm where my friend used to be a salesman. I was a salesman with them for a few months until I happened to come across another broker, whom I liked, and I decided to join him, instead. Many of the immigrants who used to remit money through us to India started saving funds for a down payment on a house. I was able to convince many of them to purchase a larger house, live on the main floor, and rent out of all the remaining areas to help pay their mortgages. Many of them were excited about their first major venture.

I worked for this broker for almost four years, mainly selling homes to new immigrants. I became a realtor for a Bengali community from India whose members believed in owning their own homes. My wife had been born in Calcutta, West Bengal, and she spoke fluent Bengali. I picked up the language while dealing with this community, which was a great asset, and I became their favourite salesperson.

As a real estate salesman selling mainly houses, I was very successful and ended up selling over 200 homes during my first four years, which was about one house per week. I was even featured in *The Toronto Star* as a successful immigrant. My reputation was impeccable, as I would never sell a home to anyone that I personally would not buy. My ability to negotiate was superb, and we very soon got over that first setback.

My typing skills helped me a lot in real estate. While most of my colleagues would show houses and get offers typed at the office, I was able to type out offers at clients' homes at the same time. This approach worked very well, as the clients did not have the time to change their minds. In one instance, I drove a couple, to see some houses in Don Mills. They liked a bungalow and wanted to make an offer. On our way back, my car developed engine trouble on the 401, and it stopped in the middle of the highway. I left my clients there and took a ride to get assistance. When I got back, I saw that an accident had taken place. My car had been hit so badly from behind that it could no longer be repaired. The police arranged for a tow truck and offered us a ride to my clients' home. The typewriter had fallen out of the trunk, but I asked the policeman if I could take it with me. The clients were disappointed because they were not sure what could be done about the bungalow. I told them, "Well, the car is gone, but that shouldn't stop us from proceeding further." Since I had the typewriter and all the necessary forms, I prepared the offer and had a taxi driver deliver it. Rather than sit back and regret what had happened, I got on with my work.

There was something else about my style of doing business that puzzled some of my colleagues: I would pick up clients and take them to see houses. Other salespeople in my office thought it to be a waste of time. They would meet their clients at the first house and have them follow him in their car or take them in his car to show another property. I told my colleagues that I picked up the clients so that I could talk to them and we could get to know each other. In other words, I first sold myself to them. Then, while dropping them off, I would talk about all the houses we had seen and try to sell them one of them. In many cases, I was able to convince them to make an offer, which I typed up on their dining room table. With this approach, I saved time in making the offers.

I kept quite busy, but I never felt tired as business was always interesting. For one thing, my wife was very helpful when it came to searching out properties, making appointments, and the like. As I said, she had come from a business family and was supportive of whatever I did. The real estate business allowed me to meet new people every single day. I also enjoyed the negotiations, and it gave me immense pleasure to satisfy my clients. When I got them a deal, they knew that I had done my best to acquire the property. This success won me many referrals from their families and friends. When I started as a salesman, however, I also started purchasing income properties, like rooming houses.

I purchased a home for us sometime in 1972. I only had a savings of about $2,000, but I was able to borrow another

$2,000 from my boss. This was how we purchased a single-family home on Broadlands Boulevard in Don Mills. It was too large for us, however, and since we didn't need all of that space, we rented the bungalow out for a short while. We moved in sometime in the middle of 1973 when we expecting our first child.

In March 1974, the government introduced the speculation tax because the sale of houses and condominium apartments had picked up steam, the prices were going up literally every day, and people were buying and immediately selling. I started doing the same, and I got a friend of mine, Lax Nagda, to join me to help me out as I was way too busy.

Together, we started buying condominiums on Dixon Road and flipping them each month. The going got tough because of the speculation tax that had been brought in. We committed to purchase twenty-four condos on Dixon Road over the next few months but did not have the funds to close all the deals. Prior to the introduction of the new tax, we had closed a couple of condos each month and making a sizable profit.

We went through some tough times as a result of the Spec Tax, however, the Canada Mortgage and Housing Corporation (CMHC) had just announced that anyone who was married with a single child and low who wanted to purchase a home could do so with only five percent down and take on a mortgage at a reasonable rate.

I studied this program thoroughly and advertised with headings like, "Are you married with one child?" We had a good response and sold a number of condos to qualified buyers. Although we didn't make much money, the scenario taught us a good lesson: one should not stretch beyond what one can handle. In other words, you can leverage an investment but do not over-leverage, as you may get stuck.

Lax and I worked with the same realtor for a few years. Lax was comfortable selling condominium apartments, but I felt that I would rather be a broker, and I started taking the necessary courses. We both left Nardi in 1976. Lax joined another broker, and I started my own company under the name of Rainbow Realty Limited.

Having settled down a bit, I started to help many of my friends and relatives to come to Canada to settle. My wife and I visited India from time to time. On one of those visits, which I believe was in 1975, there was an incident that I cannot forget.

One morning, I got up a bit early and decided to go for a walk as it was quite pleasant outside. A man came up to me and asked if I could give him two rupees because he had not eaten anything for the past two days. I handed him the money as it was not a large amount for someone coming from Canada. The man followed me for a bit and asked permission to speak further. He said that he was not a beggar, that he did not like to have to ask for help, but that he had had some bad luck. He made a living as a coolie at the local railway station, helping passengers take their baggage and boxes and delivering them wherever they went. He had a large, round basket made of bamboo that helped him carry luggage on his head.

One day, while waiting at the railway station, he dozed off. Someone stole his basket, and as he had no other means of making a living, he started to beg. He asked me if I would give him twenty-five rupees, which he would use to buy a basket and get back to his work as a coolie. I thought for a minute and gave him the twenty-five rupees, which was a substantial sum of money in those days. The man could not believe his eyes and said, "I have never met a man like you, and God will certainly do something good for you."

That evening, myself, Lata, and Manish attended our nephew's wedding. My son was about two years of age and was very playful as he went from one person to another. However, after an hour had passed in which we had not seen him, and nobody knew where he was, I started to panic. I ran from the wedding hall and started walking on the road. After I had walked for a few minutes, I saw someone coming toward me, carrying my son. I was reunited with Manish and went back to the marriage festivities. He could have been lost forever in a city like Bombay, or he could have been run over by a car, but instead, everything was fine.

It wasn't long before I remembered the man's words that morning: "God will certainly help you out." I will never forget the incident and will always do good for others.

# RAINBOW REALTY—UPS AND DOWNS

During 1976, I made up my mind to leave my employer and start my own brokerage company. It was a bit of a challenge to come up with a name for my business that most people would easily remember and with a pleasant connotation. In those days, it was common to use the name of the broker, but I didn't want to call my company Champsee Realty. A friend of mine was quite helpful, and when I thought of the name Rainbow Realty, he told me, "Mac, stop fiddling around with other names." He was right: that one sounded perfect, and it had a good rhythm to it. The choice also allowed us to make colourful signage, making it easy to remember. We once had a call from an Ottawa couple who was in Toronto for the weekend who said they saw many real estate signs, but the only one they remembered was the one with the word rainbow and the many colours, and that's why they called us.

We rented a storefront office at 1967 Lawrence Avenue East in Scarborough. I fixed up the office so it would look inviting, with the right colours and furniture. Although we had a bunch of salespeople working for us, we hardly broke even in those days. I was the president of the company, but I was also the janitor, and I used to do all of the vacuuming and cleaning on weekends. Our daughter, Sonal, was born in 1977, and my wife could devote only so much time to the business as she had two children to look after.

We managed to stay afloat for the first two years and after that, we started to make some money. In those days, we mostly sold homes, and a good part of our business came through referrals.

In 1977, I came across an individual who made a huge impact on my life. Gora Aditya, president of Med-Chem Laboratories Limited, was a great success story, and the way he started his business is very inspiring. In the early 1970s, his wife gave birth to twin boys. One day, he took her to see her doctor who ordered some lab tests. Because Gora worked in a lab at Sunnybrook Hospital, he told the doctor that he would do the blood tests and bring him the results. That was when the doctor asked him whether he would be interested in opening a small lab in the basement of his office building, saying Gora would not have to pay rent until he started making money. The idea appealed to Gora, and he invited two of his friends to invest $1,000 each so that he could start the lab. This was the beginning of Med-Chem Laboratories Limited. The business grew phenomenally, and at the height of Gora's career, he and his two partners had about six hundred people working for them.

I met Gora when I was showing some houses to his younger brother. It was obvious Gora was very successful because he was driving a big Lincoln Continental. As soon as he saw the triplex his brother was viewing, Gora encouraged him to go ahead. This response was a bit unusual, because most people, when asked for an opinion, come up with something negative or wanted to see more properties, but this man was completely positive. I later had a couple of meetings with Gora at his office, and I got him into some small mortgage investments.

One day, Gora phoned me to ask if we could go out for an informal lunch, and I was taken aback by the conversation we had over the meal. He said, point blank, "Mr. Champsee, you are really stupid." (I still address him as Mr. Aditya, and he still calls me Mr. Champsee.)

I wasn't very pleased because I was rather embarrassed by the remark. "Why do you say that?" I asked.

He observed that although I was a chartered accountant and a very educated person, I was only selling houses. I should, he said, be doing bigger and better deals, like selling land, shopping plazas, or commercial buildings. I told him that I would do that, but I did not have the necessary contacts. He then told me that in his business, he dealt with two thousand doctors, day in and day out and that he would help me by referring them to me. All he wanted in return was for me to do my utmost to give him honest advice and impeccable service. He really put Rainbow Realty on the map, and the company got a name in the real estate community for making substantially big deals because I was very capable of analyzing income properties and land and negotiating creative deals.

After he and his friends did a couple of larger deals, like an apartment building in Newmarket and a medical building in Scarborough, we decided to go forward with a seventy-three-acre parcel at the corner of Woodbine Avenue and Major Mackenzie Drive in Markham. This seventy-three-acre parcel abutted on the proposed Highway 404, which was built a few years later.

The land, which was zoned as agricultural at the time, was going to have frontage on the 404, as well as on Major Mackenzie and Woodbine. With Gora's help, Rainbow Realty did its first major syndication and purchased the land for $100,000 down, with the farmer taking back a five-year mortgage for the balance, for a total price of $520,000. The down payment was divided into $5,000 and $10,000 shares. In due course, we purchased the adjoining lands, including the corner that had been missing, for a total of about $2.2 million to Magna International. Just to give you an idea, those who had invested $10,000 in the first parcel and paid some small carrying charges received about $850,000 when the parcel was sold in 1986. Our investors from the three syndicates sold the parcel to a car manufacturer for $15.1 million. I was holidaying with my family in Vancouver when the deal was about to close, but I left them for a couple of days to return to Toronto. After I finished the deal, I went back to join them.

With Gora's help—and the help of some of his contacts—our business grew by leaps and bounds over the next few years. Our team of salespeople were good at generating a lot of business, particularly where syndicating properties with a group of investors was concerned. We would form a separate company for each syndicate and end up doing the accounting for the company as well.

Rainbow Realty did fairly well until about 1989, with the exception of a downturn for a year or two in the early 1980s, when interest rates went as high as twenty percent. Not only did we survive the downturn, we also did fairly well as we were able to get our clients into properties at bargain prices and conduct some good business in Florida, where the market was pretty buoyant. One of our salesmen, Chandrakant (Charles) Sachdev and I learned the ins and outs of doing business in Florida.

In the period from 1983 to 1985, we ran into a roadblock when one particular salesman joined us. He was good and very smooth talking, and he did a great number of deals, however, he was interested in purchasing large parcels of land around Toronto, mainly in Markham, for an overseas client. He used to work every day until late in the night, sometimes until three in the morning. He started putting so many deals together that we could hardly keep up, but a number of our salespeople got busy and found and negotiated land parcels for his client. According to him, he was purchasing all of the land for somebody connected with the sheikhs of Saudi Arabia. He was putting the deals together, getting reasonable deposits, and going ahead at full force. As a result, Rainbow Realty became very well-known among farmers and others. The land market was quite down, and it was a great time to purchase those land parcels. I did, however, get a bit worried and asked him if everything was going to be fine. He assured me everything would work out.

What this person was doing was getting a lot of smaller investors to put deposits on the various parcels that were being purchased, and then he arranged to sell everything to an overseas investor before the closings took place. A deposit of $500,000 was sent to the lawyers so that he could do this flip. Things went wrong when the overseas investor got cold feet, and in the end, Rainbow Realty was handed a lawsuit demanding the deposit back and claiming damages. Meanwhile, all of the smaller investors who had given deposits also wanted their money back. I could only salvage some deals by finding other investors, and in the end, the salesman was sent to jail. He even got one of the wardens to call me to ask if I would put up bail for him! I told the warden that this individual really belonged there and that he should just keep him there.

Our errors and omissions insurance allowed us to fight the lawsuit, and we were eventually, successful in getting ourselves out of the situation. In the end, it was proven that the salesman's actions were fraudulent, but Rainbow Realty and I were not liable for anything.

We learned a lot from this mess, and although our salespeople wasted a lot of time helping the salesman without receiving any commissions, they proved my theory that work is never wasted because we were able to utilize their knowledge and expertise in the coming years.

By then, we were finding our space on Warden Avenue rather tight, and as we were doing very well, we decided to lease over 6,000 square feet in a new office building at the corner of Victoria Park and McNicoll. We now had a great team and one of the finest brokerage offices in the city. We had a twenty-four-foot table in the boardroom, and when clients came to our office, they were immediately sold. We had pictures of some of the many commercial properties we had handled on the wall, including the land at Woodbine and Major Mackenzie, and each had a sign that read "Acquired for our Clients". These signs gave us very good exposure.

At this new office, we started syndications and joint ventures in a big way. All of the salespeople who had "wasted their time" with that salesman who could not close the deals were now well-experienced and able to put complex deals together. In those years, we put more than two hundred and fifty syndications together and did a volume of about $300 million a year.

We developed a unique method of putting the deals together. Our team of salespeople was able to select parcels of land or commercial property for the purpose of syndication. We would look at various proposals, decide to put in an offer, get an option for anywhere from a week to thirty days, and then find buyers to participate in the purchase. As the sales took place and people made money, they came back with their friends and other contacts to invest with the company, as they had developed a great deal of trust in us. Most of the deals were done right in our boardroom. Because of the level of trust, they didn't feel the need to actually go to see the property.

Similarly, when it came to reselling the property, we would sign on behalf of the investors, call a meeting, and get their agreement to sell the property for the best possible price. Many properties were resold pretty quickly. Quite a few properties were flipped by some of our salespeople and their clients. A couple of transactions stand out in my mind.

One of them involved a large acreage in Whitby near Lake Ridge Road, which someone had on option for thirty days but were short on funds to close the deal. We negotiated and paid him $1,000,000 (over and above the purchase price) for his $10,000 deposit and closed the deal. We could have resold the property for a profit, but the investors felt they would get a much better price if they were to hold onto it for a while. Another deal that I remember concerned a small strip mall on Kingston Road on which one of our salespeople had an option. He was going to drop the deal, but then he talked to me. I took three of my active salespeople with me, and after looking at the property, I decided to take the deal over for a small profit to the salesperson who had initially tied it up. We were then able to flip the property to another investor who was to close the deal on the same day. My lawyer, who had been to the closing, told me the property had been flipped five times, and that he had about seven lawyers show up for the closing because it was also being financed. I could go on with scores of examples in which many properties were flipped.

Times were great for our salespeople. A number of them made over $1,000,000 a year in commissions. One of those years, I bought Rolex watches to give to them as presents. I didn't buy one for myself, as I thought I would buy a very good one sometime later. To this day, my ex-salespeople are still wearing those watches.

Another area where there was a lot of activity was condominium apartments. As these seemed easy to understand, many people who didn't know any better started purchasing them. Even the houses in new subdivisions and re-sales were sold to hundreds of investors. None of these sales made any sense, however, because the properties were overpriced and one could not make a decent return by renting them out. Good investment properties were in short supply, and for that reason, many marginal properties were also sold.

My friend Gora—who was also a major client—ended up buying many properties. Many of our clients, whom we had advised not to buy condo apartments, went ahead and bought them anyway. Initially, as builders raised prices virtually every week, a lot of them made money flipping them. An accountant I knew, however, purchased twenty-six properties, and because he didn't have the funds to close all of them, he ended up having to declare personal bankruptcy. This, once again, teaches many of us that it is not good to bite off more than we can chew.

The market really heated up in the late 1980s due, in large measure, to investors from overseas, and we all lost sight of what was worth buying. Every Tom, Dick, and Harry was talking of nothing but real estate and the big money that somebody could make. We seemed to forget the saying, "Do not buy when everybody is buying." We, unfortunately, were caught in this cycle. Most of us lost a lot of money and were taught a very tough lesson.

The 1990s saw one of the greatest downturns in the real estate history of Toronto and its surroundings. A lot of people purchased properties beyond their means because they all thought someone else would buy them and they would earn a profit. I also took a proprietary interest in many joint ventures. At the height of the market at the start of 1990, I was into about sixty syndicates. Our monthly overhead, including payments on the various deals and the cost of running a large office, was over $125,000.

Because we lost money each month, we had to move to a smaller office, first on Woodbine and then on Esna Park in Markham. Our sales force also got smaller. It was really a test of time, and I was advised by my lawyers and accountants to declare bankruptcy so that all our difficulties would come to an end. However, I made up my mind that I was not going to do that. I was prepared to face all my problems to resolve them as best I could. The thought of bankruptcy just did not sit well with me. I knew, from experience, that the financial misery would come to an end at some point and that I would start doing well again. Besides, a person who has gone bankrupt always carries a stigma.

Many of our syndicate members—who generally had no problem meeting the monthly payments—failed to make them now. Some of them simply decided to take a walk rather than continue to make payments. Other investors took over their interests and started to make payments for themselves and others.

The market was going downhill by the day, and none of the properties was moving. Many tenants in our shopping plazas were also in trouble, and many of them were either making lower rental payments or not making payments at all. A lot of them had to declare bankruptcy. We simply took a walk from eight or nine shopping plaza strips, losing all of the equity in the process.

Again, we were not the only ones losing money. Large and astute corporations, such as Olympia and York, had to declare bankruptcy. Many smaller trust companies failed while many developers ceased to operate. It was a bloodbath everywhere. Quite a few office buildings in downtown Toronto sold for as low as $10 per square foot, land and building! I know a building in Don Mills that was purchased by someone in good times for about $26 million but which was sold for a measly $2.5 million. Those people who had money and foresight made a lot of money down the road.

We were very upfront with our clients, and although many had their grievances and many lost huge amounts of capital, we did not face a single lawsuit from them as we had not misled any of them. We all lost because of the market, and we did not knowingly entice them into any bad deals. We also lost a number of salesmen, but most of the key people remained with me. All of these people knew I did not create the downturn in the market, and that I could not avert the crisis. We could not control the economy; the whole country was going through a recession.

The downturn continued until about 1995 when the market gradually started to pick up, and those investors who still had funds to invest were able to get the best possible deals.

A number of joint ventures in which some investors had to sign personally, ran into trouble as there wasn't the cash flow to meet the mortgage payments, and many lawsuits ensued. I am going to highlight some of these lawsuits because I had to face them over the next few years.

# 5
# LAWSUITS AND MORE LAWSUITS

Rainbow Realty went through a rather difficult time in the mid-1990s. Many of our investors—including ourselves— were not very solvent. For this reason, a number of our bank loans and mortgages went into default. Many investors simply took a walk from their equity, leaving the mortgage companies to deal with the properties. Some investors had to declare bankruptcy in order to relieve themselves of the aggravation.

Rather than declare personal bankruptcy, I wanted to find my way out of my financial mess by negotiating with each and every one of my creditors. I had loans or mortgages from the Royal Bank, TD Canada Trust, Imperial Life, and others. When it came to the land, the original owners had, in most cases, taken back mortgages which had not carried personal guarantees. When the investors took a walk from the investments, the original owners simply foreclosed on the property and took back ownership. I recall that our group took a walk from thirty-six properties in the first thirty-six months after the start of the downturn, about one property per month, but there were many more casualties. I lost over eighty percent of my net worth during those years.

I approached many of our creditors and asked if they would give us some relief to make payments we could afford and look after the balance in the future. If the economy improved, they wouldn't lose any money. Some of them were willing to make deals, taking so much on a dollar and writing-off the balance. Most of the larger financial institutions were reluctant to make any deals.

I was faced with some lawsuits, most of which were due to my inability to meet payments on all the loans, and I had to engage a litigation lawyer to protect me. (Fortunately, Lata had not signed personally on anything.) I remembered that a few years back, a lawyer had sued me on something very flimsy. I had initially laughed at the lawsuit, but in the end, I lost, though, fortunately, the amount was not that big. I decided that if anyone could help me out, it would be Don Crabbe, that particular lawyer.

I approached Don and explained my situation, and as a result, he handled all of the lawsuits. (There were more than twenty.) He suggested I see a trustee in bankruptcy, which I did. One of the accountants in the firm that looked after our business specialized in such matters, and he could see that I did not have enough funds to meet all my obligations.

With Don's help, I started to deal with the institutions. Because each of them had very deep pockets, they could go on fighting with me for the next few years. Don, however, started questioning them on their calculations, bookkeeping, management, and many other items. In some cases, it was really hilarious. Many of the institutions were rather large, and often the left hand did not know what the right hand was doing. Things went wrong in many instances because the property managers either did not do a good job or had far too much to handle. Let me elaborate on some of the lawsuits Don handled.

One of the insurance companies had a mortgage on a project in Newmarket. We had several investors, and we were required to sign on the transfer of the first mortgage, which was around $1,000,000. (The project was syndicated for $2.7 million.) As time was tight, I signed personally for the first mortgage, thinking that if I got called on making the payment, I wouldn't mind taking over the project for that mortgage amount. However, values really dwindled in the downturn. I had demands for monthly payments to the first mortgagee, and I told them that we could not make full payments as the rental income had come down. We offered to manage the property because we were very familiar with the tenancies and the shortfall was not that large. The mortgage company did not agree and did not want our help. They informed all of the tenants of the change and started to collect the rent. The tenants took advantage of the lax management, and in the end, the mortgage company brought our monthly income of about $9,000 down to less than $3,000. As a consequence, the mortgage shortfalls grew larger.

Don questioned them on everything they had done and asked them to submit a proper accounting in a form we could understand. For some reason, many such companies are not well-equipped to deal with the nitty-gritty details, and this one kept making mistakes. Don was able to question them on every little thing. For example, he would select a tenant and ask the company exactly when the rental payments were made. They often didn't know the answers to such questions because the property managers had a lot of properties to oversee, each of which was in trouble with various mortgage institutions. The lawsuit went on for more than three years. I was being sued for more than $1,000,000, but then Don told me that they wanted the matter settled. We decided to offer them a measly sum of $10,000; the next thing we heard was that they had settled and closed the file. Many of the companies had provided for such losses by budgeting certain amounts every year, and they had to clear their books of non-performing loans.

We also had a project of retail spaces and apartments near Bloor and Lansdowne. There was a first mortgage of $2 million that did not have any personal guarantees. The project ran into trouble, and I approached the institution to see if it would write off the loan to $1.5 million and capitalize on some of the interest. They did not go for it, wanting, instead, to manage the project. The project was rather messy because it was not properly constructed and the property was in a rather bad area with a lot of drug users, so I advised them that handling the project themselves would not be in their interest. They did not listen, however, and the result was turmoil.

After they had spent over two years as property managers, I got a call from them one day, and we settled everything for $400,000 in cash. The project was given back to us in a disastrous state, with tenants who were not paying and more vacancies, problems that cost us money each month. We had to spend a lot of time and money to put it back on even ground. Finally, we were so fed up that we sold the project to an investor one of my salespeople had brought to me. We broke even, or perhaps made a small amount of money, and to date, the same investor is doing fine with the project.

Don also helped me with some other legal matters. We had three different lawsuits from a trust company that had financed an industrial complex. The suits went on for a very long time due to Don's innovative ways. We both could see the benefit of dragging things out in order to tire the other party out, and Don did a great job of it. The trust company finally got tired of the process, accepted five cents on the dollar, and called it a day. I would have gladly paid them more if they had agreed to it earlier in the game. My bank was also not receptive to the idea of taking losses in the three lawsuits they filed against me, but Don helped me out again, and everything was settled with them.

The lawsuits taught me a lot. I found that the courts in Canada are very fair and make sure that everything is above board. Although we had to make settlements and payments in order to get a clean slate, it was well worth it. My credit rating remained impeccable even when I could not make all the payments in their entirety.

Looking back at that period from 1972 to 1989, I see that, in general, there was a rise in real estate values and that we were able to take advantage as we went along. Then, in the 1990s, we faced a storm, but we did not give up. Anybody can be a pilot in calm weather; it is the storm that tests a pilot. Given the turmoil in our business, my wife and I have experienced stressful periods, however, Lata is someone who never panics, and neither of us gets bogged down by challenges that seem insurmountable. We try to find solutions, rather than ranting about the problems.

By the mid-1990s, we were carrying on with our business on a much smaller scale, though some of my key people stayed with me. It all changed, however, when I changed my career for a brief period. An overseas investor who had come to Canada on a business visa met me and asked me to find him a pharmaceutical manufacturing facility that would employ a few people. It was not an easy order, as such companies seldom come up for sale in an open market. However, being as persistent as I am, I found one, and I am happy to cover that story in the next chapter.

# PHARMACEUTICAL MANUFACTURING

While I was in crisis in mid-1995, a friend's son, who had recently obtained a visa, came to Canada. The terms of the visa dictated he purchase an active business to employ local people. He told me their organization in India was most interested in pharmaceuticals. I suggested he leave the matter with me because pharmaceutical businesses did not usually show up on our real estate listings. He also told me he had been able to get one of his employees to Canada and that the employee was technically qualified and experienced in pharmaceutical manufacturing.

I certainly had a task in front of me. Real estate was very slow, but I had been given the opportunity to make a decent commission. I just had to find a pharmaceutical company for my client to buy, but I had no idea how to go about it. I started by talking to some of my friends who were pharmacists and who bought their supplies from manufacturers. I found out that one of the large distributors, Drug Trading Company Limited, which had been incorporated in 1895, had a small manufacturing division known as the Druggists' Corporation that had been incorporated in 1932. By coincidence, they had a factory on Pharmacy Avenue.

I approached the manager and asked if his principals would be interested in importing Vitamin E from India as my client was producing it in a factory there. We spent some time looking into this possibility, but it did not go anywhere. Then, I wanted to know if the principals would consider a joint venture with us in the manufacturing arm of their business. We knew they needed money because they had overextended themselves in their core business, which was the supply of pharmaceuticals to pharmacies.

After months of going back and forth, we were at the negotiating table with the owners of the company. At that point, they were interested in selling off their manufacturing facility. We were able to agree on a price and as well as a supply agreement in which they bought a certain number of pharmaceutical products from us. However, we ended up buying it lock, stock, and barrel for some $2 million, which included the building on Pharmacy Avenue along with the manufacturing facility, all Drug Identification Numbers (DIN), their licences to produce, and an experienced staff. I knew this was a great price because the company was making money, unlike its parent company, which lost money every year. Nobody paid much attention to this fact as they were all busy looking after the parent company's problems. As an accountant, I saw the potential.

It took about six months of negotiation before we were ready to go forward. I called my investor, but he said that he could not come from India as other important matters were keeping him busy. He appointed me vice president of the company, wired the necessary funds, and we closed the deal and hired the existing staff and the manager to carry on with us.

Neither my wife nor I knew how to run a pharmaceutical company, but she was very interested as she liked working in the production of pharmaceuticals, most of which involved repackaging over-the-counter medications and making cough syrups and other common remedies. She liked the idea of production, which was very different from the real estate business. When the investor came over to see everything, I told him that I had done my job and my commission for the deal was $100,000. When he said they would not pay me anything, I was taken aback. He then said he wanted me to have a carried interest of twenty percent in the company with no financial investment from me and a salary with which I would be happy. They also made the deal more palatable by specifying that I could carry on with my real estate dealings. I was reluctant to take something over about which I knew nothing, but my wife encouraged me to move forward as we were making no money in real estate.

By that time we had lost many of our salespeople and decided to close the company offices in Markham. Although I did not feel good about closing the operation, it was the prudent thing to do as the business was not generating enough cash flow to pay all the bills.

Although we did not know how to run a manufacturing operation, we used our common sense and started saving money where we could, for example, in the purchase of supplies, bottles, cartons, and the like. Because of everything we did, we made a profit of over $1.7 million in the first year on an investment of $2 million, which made our investors very happy. I received a fair compensation and a very decent salary on top of what my wife was able to make.

In spite of everything, I did carry on with some real estate operations, happy to make deals while the company was going full blast. The investors did not object to my using their offices to see clients for real estate matters.

One particularly interesting situation arose during these years. I knew a farmer in Stouffville who had a large farm on Ninth Line. He had conditionally sold his farm to some investors who were handling everything through their lawyers. He was selling off ninety acres of his hundred-acre farm and was working through the severance procedures, which was taking longer than he had anticipated. In the meantime, he had to continue paying the mortgage—on which he had started defaulting—and he was close to mortgage foreclosure. The lawyers kept getting extension after extension on the closing, in an attempt to tire the farmer out so they could buy the property through the mortgage foreclosure. He was selling the entire ninety acres for only $740,000, and he asked me to purchase the property to get him out of his mess. I said that I would, but only if we got a clearance with the first deal (I only wanted to work through the salesperson who had been involved in the transaction as she would look after the farmer's interests). One day, I got a call from the salesperson in which she stated that their present deal was off. She then asked me if I would make an offer of $900,000 for the same parcel, given that they had incurred many expenses in obtaining the severance. In the deal that had been struck through the investors' lawyers, the total consideration was $740,000. I made out a clean, one-page offer, and the farmer accepted it in the presence of his lawyers.

A few days later, I got a call from the salesperson's lawyers who said that I had interfered with their deal, but I was not afraid. By that time, I had been through many lawsuits, and one more was not going to shake me up. A few days later, I was offered $200,000 to get out of the deal. I decided to register a *lis pendens*, (lawsuit pending) and pay the land transfer tax. The other party also registered a lis pendens, and that was how the property was sold twice. I consulted Don Crabbe who told me it was a good case, and I demanded they pay me $500,000 to get out of the deal as well as to pay the present owner $900,000 for his land. The matter went to court, and in the end, the other side had to settle by paying me a total of $450,000, and the farmer got $900,000 instead of $740,000. The settlement amount came in handy as I was building my dream home at the time.

We continued with the manufacturing of pharmaceuticals for some time but then told our investors that we wanted out of the venture because it was not something that kept my interest, nor was I doing justice to the job. I am wheeler-dealer in millions of dollars, but in pharmaceuticals, we had to negotiate to look for penny savings. It was not a field for which I was cut out, as I had had no knowledge of or training for it. The investor told me that I should look for a buyer. They were prepared to make a small profit or even take a loss, as they decided they did not really want to settle in Canada by then; they were too busy overseas.

Fortunately, I found myself an opportunity. As it turned out, the parent company from which we had purchased the business was not manufacturing anything at the time, and they had an image problem since the company could not very well say they were manufacturing the drugs sold to the pharmacies affiliated with them. All the board members who had made a decision to sell us the operation were fired because they were not doing a good job for the shareholders. The president of the new board called me into his office one day to ask if we would consider selling the company back to them. I said yes, because I had that authority, and he asked me how much we would want.

Without blinking an eye, I told him that we wanted to sell it for $10 million. He laughed at the figure and said, "Mac, you just bought this for a song, and now you want $10 million? This is too much."

I told him that when I bought the company I was crazy but that having been in the business and coming to understand its potential, I could see that it was worth a lot more. I suggested the president have his chief financial officer go through everything at our company. In the meantime, I prepared a booklet in which I set out all of the facts and figures.

Being such an old company, it had licences to manufacture tablets with codeine and many other medicines, most of them over-the-counter. In all, they had about 140 DINs. Since it took a fair amount of time to obtain each of these numbers from Health Canada, they were worth a lot.

Within the next few weeks, we had made a deal. The price was $6 million for the business and equipment, and we were to own the building. They wanted to rent it, which suited us just fine. Eventually, when the lease expired, we were able to sell the building for $2 million. In summary, the investment of $2 million grew to $8 million, and I was free as a bird once more. I had been eager to relieve myself of a business that was making me depressed, and we were able to get out with flying colours.

However, we didn't stop there. My investors did not need all of the funds back in their home country, and they were happy to invest them through me. That was how I purchased some apartment buildings in Niagara Falls, Hamilton, and Toronto. All of the investments had the potential to create more income, and therefore, offer better value if we made certain physical improvements. When we were able to convert the rental buildings in Niagara Falls into condominium buildings, the investment paid off very handsomely.

# 7
# LESSONS LEARNED

In the twenty years we were in business, we had many ups and downs. We persevered through the heated markets of 1973-74, 1980, and 1989 that were followed by downturns, making many gains and suffering many losses. Each of these experiences taught us lessons that you cannot find in any book. There is no simple way to learn: you just have to deal with circumstances as they unfold. The following is a summary of things we learned that helped us to avoid repeating our mistakes. In other chapters, I will illustrate them in more detail.

As earlier chapters make clear, time you may think of as wasted is never really wasted if it provides an experience that you need. There were many activities on which, for one reason or another, we spent what seemed to be too much time, but we were eventually able to use what we had learned from them.

Success in real estate is about adding value. Each time we purchased a property and improved it by completing all the necessary and cosmetic repairs, we ended up further ahead. In fact, the results were generally much better than we anticipated. Our apartment buildings in downtown Toronto, Scarborough, Willowdale, and many others areas generated good profits due to the added value of re-modeling and improvements made.

We learned not to bite off more than we could chew. In other words, we learned not to burden ourselves with liabilities that we couldn't handle in the event of a downturn. This is what happened in 1973-74 when we purchased a number of condominium apartments of which we had a rough time getting out. Similarly, we ran into huge problems in 1989, as we had acquired far too many properties, mostly undeveloped land, which did not provide a cash flow.

We also learned that one should not own too many properties that do not produce a cash flow. This is what really went wrong in the late 1980s. Because we owned far too much in the way of raw land—which did not produce any income—we could not maintain our monthly payments, and ultimately had to take a walk from some of our properties. Owning land is good, but it can be very cumbersome when there are no other sources of positive cash flow.

Learning how to borrow is another very important lesson that we learned through experience. If funds are borrowed wisely, they really pay off. Leverage is good because it allows you to go much further, faster. Well-managed income properties allowed us to pull out substantial funds by refinancing, and as a result, we were able to acquire more properties with a limited down payment.

In addition, owning only your home may not be the wisest idea. No matter how high its value goes, you will never make money, because you will always require a place to live. It's the next property—which could be an apartment, a townhouse, a house, a small apartment building, or a bunch of stores—that helps you make money.

We also learned to believe in our products. We came across many sales professionals who made millions upon millions of dollars for their clients and were satisfied with the commissions. It seemed that, for some reason, they never believed in their own product. We did very well as we tried to get an interest in the many syndications that we were forming, and we had the benefit of that interest. We did, however, get carried away, owning much more than we could handle, and suffered some losses as a result.

Another lesson is that it pays to fight lawsuits. It is said that most lawsuits die a premature death because, in most cases, they are settled before they go to trial. Understanding this reality helped me personally because I saved huge sums of money. There are always some areas where lawyers can make a case for you so that you either do not pay the amount at all or you settle the case for a greatly reduced sum.

We also learned that persistence always pays off—it was what really helped our people make money. Generally speaking, anyone who gives up prematurely ends up with the short end of the stick.

Having good accountants, lawyers, and other professionals to guide you is of the utmost importance in business, we discovered. The advice and guidance that one can get from professionals can be helpful, and it generally comes at a significantly low cost.

It is important to know that taking risks is necessary to get ahead and achieve something in life. You can analyze something but cannot always be one hundred percent sure about everything. This is why we apply the Rule of Ninety Percent when we are deciding whether to do a deal. If you are ninety percent satisfied with a project, then you should take a chance and go ahead with it. It is very difficult to make a perfect deal when one party has to compromise and still be satisfied with the outcome.

# 8
# WHY REAL ESTATE?

As I explained in an earlier chapter, when Samir and I arrived in Canada in July 1965, we spent about two weeks in Montreal before travelling to Toronto, where we stayed at a downtown hotel while trying to find a place to live. We looked for places in the Annex area as it was popular with new immigrants in those days, and there were many rooming houses from which to choose.

While looking for signs, we came across a place on Walmer Road. As I indicated earlier, this was when we met Herb Mackenzie, the landlord, who had visited India and Burma as an air force pilot during World War II. He offered us a large room with cooking facilities, which seemed to suit us well. We felt very comfortable there and decided to rent the room.

Herb became very friendly with us, and from time to time, invited us to his apartment at the back of the house. He talked of the days he had spent in India and Burma during the war, and he even spoke a bit of Hindi.

One evening, when Samir and I were sitting with Herb in his living room sipping tea, he looked at me, smiled, and said, "You know, Mac, I've been to India and Burma as an air force pilot during the Second World War. I can even speak a few words in your language: *'Kaise ho'*? Meaning, how are you?" We chuckled and clapped in appreciation, and Herb threw his head back and enjoyed a laugh. Occasionally, we had some good parties.

That evening I asked, "Herb, what exactly do you do?"

He looked straight into my eyes, smiled, took a sip from his teacup, placed his elbows on the armrests, relaxed, and explained, "Look, my friends: my wife and I own this house. We rent the ten furnished rooms like yours. We do all the cleaning and collect rent weekly. After paying the mortgage, realty taxes, and maintenance expenses, we have some money left over."

He then leaned forward. "Mac, here is my advice to you: if you want to be successful in Canada, you should get into real estate."

It was as if he could see my future. It did not excite me then, but it did plant a seed in the back my mind. Little did I know then that one day, that was exactly what I would be doing. I liked the idea as it was a business that could run on its own and make money in the long-term because property values keep on going up, and so does rent.

About a year later, Samir and I had saved about $1,000. He had been working at the University of Toronto Libraries, and the university had started a credit union for its employees and was offering a $5,000 loan to any member who wanted to purchase a house. We discussed it and then talked to Herb.

Herb helped us find a ten-room house on Kendal Avenue, the next street over, and we purchased it in 1966 with a total down payment of $6,000, made up of our savings of $1,000 and $5,000 borrowed from the credit union. The total price of the house was $30,400.

We started to do a lot of work on the house, renovating it, doing minor repairs, cleaning, painting, and decorating. We did most of the work ourselves. Not only were we now living for free, but there was some money left over every month after we paid the mortgage and all of the other expenses. I thought it was a terrific business, particularly suited to new immigrants like us. Many of our friends and acquaintances were curious as to how we managed it. In those days, many of them didn't even know what a mortgage was, however, a lot of them wanted to do what we had.

One day, a friend of ours came to visit us with a real estate salesman, named Zack. He showed our house to Zack and then the friend showed us the house he intended to buy. I went to look at the house and advised the friend to purchase it. Zack called me over to the side and told me that he would give me a referral fee if he ended up selling the house to our friend. The next thing I knew, he'd sent me the sum of $225, which was a huge amount, as I was making only about $300 per month at my job.

Zack told me that if I helped him when necessary, he would give me a referral fee, depending on the value of the houses sold to the clients. This arrangement lasted for a few years, and it served us well. I made up my mind that, one day, I would simply get into real estate as the business really appealed to me.

I graduated as a chartered accountant in 1971, though I continued to work with my employer at an annual salary of $12,000, which was considered pretty good pay in those days. However, one day in 1972, I decided that I would quit and become a real estate salesman. Many of my colleagues laughed at me, saying, "Mac, you are a chartered accountant, and now you work with housewives, discussing kitchens and bathrooms." I did, however, leave and made $35,000 in my first full year at real estate, which was far more than what my colleagues did.

That was how I got into real estate, and I have never looked back since!

# KNOWLEDGE IS POWER
# AND EXPERIENCE IS AN INVALUABLE ASSET

Experience cannot be obtained by reading books or listening to other people. Rather, you need to take a very active role in your own life.

In the previous chapter, I explained how we ended up purchasing the rooming house at 122 Kendal Avenue in 1966. As owners, we came to know a great deal about real estate prices, mortgages, operations, income and expenses, tenant issues, and property maintenance. We also gained a lot in terms of experience and knowledge.

My dealings with Zack not only earned me money that I badly needed in those days, but they also opened my eyes to the possibilities in real estate. As well, my work as an auditor gave me a chance to look at the books and records of many clients, some of which were making good money in real estate. I have already told the story of one such client who had purchased a farm for $32,000 from a mortgage company, and in 1971, after getting the zoning changed to residential, sold it for $1 million.

The knowledge of the real estate industry that I gained as an auditor was invaluable, and I decided that one day I would get into the real estate business because it would change my future.

As I think of my work as a chartered accountant, I recall the discussion I had with my father when I was deciding whether to study engineering. As I noted earlier, my father was adamant that he would not pay for my education if I planned to work for somebody else. He'd told me, "If you want to study business, I will help." As a chartered accountant, I could only make a certain amount for every hour worked. There was only one way to make more money, and that was to work hard for as many hours as I could manage. It is difficult to get rich when you are being paid by the hour because you cannot work more than say, ten hours a day. Real estate was very different: my income depended on the deals I made. In my first year, I made more money than well-qualified professionals in highly respected fields, and I never looked back.

Because my father understood the concept of business and its money-making potential, I am sure he would have interested in the work of Robert Kiyosaki, author of *Rich Dad, Poor Dad*. In it, Kiyosaki describes a situation in which students A and B work in businesses owned by students C and D. C and D, who are academically average, make handsome profits, even after paying A and B, because their businesses give them leverage. If a person has no leverage, there is only so much money that person can earn. Kiyosaki points out that there is something off about our education system and our society. Smart people—students A and B students in *Rich Dad* parlance—rush into professions that seem to pay well but demand a lot of time for the income they make. In other words, jobs that offer no leverage. Enterprising students—the Cs and Ds—realize that they cannot get into prestigious programs and thus will have no career to "fall back on," however, they understand the concept of leverage. They create opportunities and wind up having people work for them.

Our society idolizes doctors and lawyers as high achievers and considers them highly paid people, but the fact is that even the very best doctor has an upper-income limit because there are only so many hours in a day and therefore, only so many procedures a doctor can perform. If, however, the doctor owns a medical business, then he can enjoy leverage.

The irony is that people in these professions rarely run successful businesses because they overthink them and don't delegate the work, thereby leveraging the business. Very often, the most successful medical businesses are owned by people who are not medically qualified specialists. They do, however, are aware of what they do not know and hire the best specialists to run the business for them. They also know how to delegate, take advantage of leverage, and maximize their returns.

Looking back, I can see that if I had gone my way, I would have made a good engineer at best. However, one day back in 1988, at the height of my career in real estate, I counted five engineers working for me as salespeople. These people found better opportunities in real estate and left engineering to start selling properties as a result. In other words, they, too, had discovered the power of leverage.

Today, given my portfolio of apartment buildings, I hire engineers to supervise major renovations. Over the past fifteen years, I have awarded contracts exceeding $20 million for work on various buildings, and I have hired very smart engineers to supervise the work. I have benefitted from the activities of all these engineers—talk about leverage!

My father was so right.

# 10
# WORK IS NEVER WASTED

It is very typical for people to say, "I don't want to waste any time," or "I don't want to waste your time or mine." When something doesn't work out, it is also typical for them to say, "That was a complete waste of time." Unfortunately, in real estate, it seems that a vast amount of time simply appears to be unproductive. Deals may not materialize, or clients may change their minds for one reason or another.

Looking back over my life, I have come to the conclusion that "time" we believe is wasted is rarely a write-off. I have coined a saying: work is never wasted. Anything you do, even if it gets you nowhere, can teach you what not to do in future or give you an insight into something else, if you are willing to learn. Let me give you some real-life examples.

Around the year 2000, a salesman of mine called me to say that he knew of an apartment building in the Yonge-Eglinton corridor owned by partners who were constantly fighting. He told me that the building might be for sale, and if I was interested, he could arrange a meeting with the president of the title-holding entity. He also provided me with enough details to pique my interest.

I met the president, and he stated that there were seventeen partners in the venture. There was no buy-sell agreement in place, which meant that although the majority of the partners wanted to sell the building, they were not able to because ten or fifteen percent of the owners would not agree. I told the president that I would send him a letter about our meeting and our interest in acquiring the building and that he could call me whenever they were ready. At first glance, my efforts might have seemed like a total waste of time, however, this was not the case.

About six years later, I got a call from the property manager, who said they were ready to sell; all of the partners had come to an agreement. When I met with him, he showed me other brokers' opinions of its market value. I told him that our group was interested and that we would prepare an offer, but I would not charge a commission because the deal would be looked after by our group. Ultimately, we made a deal for a purchase price of $3 million. I syndicated the property among four parties, one of them my daughter, Sonal. When the news circulated, I had about four calls from other brokers asking how we had bought the property at such an attractive price.

The story doesn't end there.

Six years after that, with sound management and appropriate renovations, Sonal was able to bring the operating income substantially up. Because the market had also improved, the property was resold at $8,225,000—all cash—thereby making a handsome profit! As is clear, the work wasn't wasted. Rather, it paid us tremendous rewards.

My success in the United States also strengthened my belief in the value of learning from experience. From the time I became involved in real estate, I was aware that many new immigrants like myself had come from tropical climates and would not like Canada's harsh winters as they grew older. With this idea in mind, I started pursuing some land deals in Florida in 1977. After two or three years of work (on and off), though I had achieved nothing, I was, nevertheless, ahead of the curve. It might have seemed that my efforts were a total waste of time and money, they weren't.

In the early 1980s, I approached General Development Corporation, which had just one broker in Toronto marketing Florida lots. They made me their agent as I was very familiar with retirement communities in Florida and—bingo! My salespeople and I sold over two hundred lots and made quite a bit of money at a time when the market in Toronto was not very good.

My dealings in Florida, acting on my own behalf and as the agent for General Development Corporation, paid us more rewards in the early 1980s when the Toronto market tanked due to high-interest rates. As well, Charles was able to persuade an overseas client of his to go to Florida, and the work I had already done meant I was very familiar with the real estate there. We did more than ten deals in Vero Beach and made huge commissions as they were all fairly large transactions.

Sometime in the 1980s, another hardworking salesman of mine started looking at real estate in Texas, which was doing very badly. Savings and loan associations had many properties on their hands that needed to be unloaded. He attended some of their auctions and kept in close contact with the government employees in charge of the inventory. When he came across a three-hundred-and-thirty-acre parcel of land just north of Dallas, he thought it made sense to do a deal. The negotiations with the government went on for many months, and when the deal was just about to close, he approached us as he did not have anyone for the project. It seemed to him then that he might have wasted all of his time, but his efforts paid off for him and for us.

I talked to one of my salespeople, Charles Sachdev, whom I mentioned earlier because he had some overseas clients, and they were very interested. As a result, all of us, including the client, flew to Dallas to complete the deal. The land in question had a first mortgage of over $18 million, and our client purchased it for about $2.7 million, yielding us handsome fees. The client is still holding onto the parcel, which is worth at least $50 million in the current market.

The lessons I learned in the States also helped me advise my son when he was living in San Francisco. In 2005, the housing market heated up in that city, and I wanted to try to make a good deal in a bad market. I came across several ads advertising properties with tenants in common (TIC) when going through the classified ads in the newspapers. I also took advice from a lawyer who helped me understand TICs and successfully converted a property. This is how we ended up owning a property with four apartments. Three of them were sold for a good profit, and those sales resulted in a much better deal for the fourth property, which is owned by my son. It's a million-dollar property that only cost him about half the price. Today, it is worth close to two million dollars.

A relationship I developed some years ago also supports my point about the ways in which the investment of time can ultimately pay off. I came to know someone representing overseas investors from Africa. He had been talking to many commercial realtors but did not buy anything. I had a hard time getting him to make a purchase, so I stopped paying him much attention. However, the gentleman would call me after he looked at some projects to ask for my opinion. I gave it religiously, but I still did not make any deals with him. He became well-known among commercial brokers as someone who analyzed project after project but would not commit to a deal. Several brokers asked why I wasted my time with him when, in fact, I was not wasting time. Here was a well-educated person feeding me his analyses of properties. In a sense, I was getting his work for free. I also ended up making a few deals on the properties he did not buy, because he could never justify the price or the location.

With our broad experience owning and managing low-income properties and developing connections in Toronto, I ended up on the City's Affordable Housing Committee. I was introduced to Paul Tamale at one of the meetings. Tamale, who was originally from Tanzania, became my right-hand man in many projects. Once more, this experience proves that none of my time was ever really wasted.

If my stories do not convince you, here are two more anecdotes that might help persuade you.

Albert Einstein was working on a project, and he seemed to be wasting a lot of time as he tried to show positive results and failed about four thousand times, however, on the four thousand and first time, he succeeded. When someone asked him about the time he had "wasted", he had this to say: "I know now what not to do for the first four thousand times and what exactly to do now." He finally succeeded in the project big time and never regretted the time it took.

We can also look at the story of Thomas Edison as told by Napoleon Hill, the writer of the monumental self-improvement book *Think and Grow Rich*. Edison tried more than ten thousand times to make the first, workable, incandescent light bulb. He did not regret any of his failed attempts, which others might see as a great waste of time. He saw each try as the potential to make a light bulb, and he eventually succeeded and made a fortune.

Never regret the time you invest in your business, my friends, even if you initially do not make any money, because this is the way the world works. If you persist, if you just keep doing the work, you will one day succeed and be rewarded.

# HOW EXPERTS COMPLICATE SIMPLE CRITERIA

Investing in real estate is just simple arithmetic, however, experts in the industry seem to complicate it by their analyses of trends, cap rates, internal rates of return on investment and the like, almost none of which is properly understood by most investors. Those who are successful seem to follow their gut feelings and do some simple math when deciding on any given project.

Whether you are going to purchase a single-family home, a six-plex or a multi-storeyed building, you don't need more than a simple $10 calculator. You don't need to understand the economy, follow trends, or read newspaper articles. You don't need advice from so-called experts who may never have owned anything besides their homes or cottages. If you are planning to buy apartment buildings or other income properties, listen to other owners rather than the consultants. There is, of course, no harm in reading newspapers or listening to speeches, as long as you follow your gut feelings.

Your analysis of a real estate investment should not take more than one page of calculations and a thorough visit to the project. You do, of course, need some cash in your pocket and/or a decent line of credit. Most of the time, you don't require much money if you have equity in other projects. Remember that you don't need to buy your own home as a first step. If you have the means, you can buy a home and arrange a good line of credit, especially if the market value of the home justifies it.

As I have explained, my first real estate sales contact was the real estate salesman in the early 1970s who said that if you know how to add and subtract, most of the work is already done, because all you need to do is add up the income and deduct the expenses. The bottom line should tell you if anything remains after mortgage payments.

There are, of course, some key things to consider. Look at the potential of the project. Are present rents too low? Are expenses too high, and if so, can they be reduced? What can be done to make the project a success over the next three years? Look at the vacancy rates in the building and in the neighbouring ones. How could you make your building a good place to live and could you save on expenses by, for example, changing the toilets to low-flow types, replacing windows and roofs, and generally making the building energy efficient? Your answers will tell you a lot. Don't get bogged down by cap rates because real estate deals are not like lab tests in that they do not produce the same results each time. Cap rates can change significantly if the area and all other attributes are good.

I could provide many examples of the ways simple addition and subtraction can pay off. For example, we purchased a run-down, eighty-five-year-old building on Roehampton Avenue for about $3 million with barely a six-cap, a term I will explain in more detail later. Because the building suffered from a lack of maintenance and proper management, the average rentals were too low for the area. With significant improvements over the following five years, the building more than doubled in value, and the return was over triple the down payment. The building fetched over $8 million when sold, a remarkable return given that we had purchased it for only $3 million.

On Midland Avenue, we bought two, totally run-down buildings, the result of bad management and deferred maintenance over a span of almost forty years. With renovations and energy-saving measures, the buildings looked more like condos when it was sold three years later, providing a very decent return.

I could give dozens of other concrete examples that show it is important to look at the potential of a property and not just its history, which is simply a guideline. It is really important not to get bogged down in the details but to focus on the future. Warren Buffett famously said, "If you are a farmer, why worry about what analysts have to say about the prospects for your farm? It's your farm. You work it. It doesn't matter what the analysts say. You get to decide how well it will do."

It is also important to follow your intuition, to trust your inner voice and go with your gut. If you listen to your heart instead of everyone else, you will make the right decision. Don't complicate things that don't need to be complicated. Surround yourself with good contractors and reasonably priced, efficient workers.

To some, my words may sound like mere positive thinking. To the mystic, success has to do with putting out an intention and compelling the universe to bring that intention to physical manifestation. I know from experience that when I make up my mind about what I want to accomplish in a particular year and work on it, I have always achieved my goals.

# YOU DON'T NEED TO BE "SMART" TO MAKE MONEY

Many (book) smart people don't make big money. Most of the time, they spend an unnecessary amount of time analyzing data and following theoretical ideas that don't help them achieve significant financial rewards. One doesn't need to have book smarts to be successful. I have met many wealthy individuals whom I didn't think were particularly clever, yet they had made it all the way.

Persistence is what makes someone successful. Persistence pays. Persistent people don't give up. Rather, they set a goal, pursue it, and keep working at it. I am but one of them—I have come across many others like-minded people over the course of my life.

One man who worked for me for about twenty years, someone I have already mentioned, is Charles Sachdev. His best quality is persistence. He simply does not give up on anything, and he is willing to face disappointment in the process. He ended up doing better than many of my "smarter" colleagues in the long run. If he had a client, he kept talking to him on and off, making sure he never annoyed him. Once he decided on a project, he would never give up on it, and it paid off in most cases. For example, he learned of a strip mall near Markham and Sheppard was for sale, and he kept making offers until he finally developed the deal to the point at which someone else could take over and close it. He repeatedly told me that there was definitely a Chinese investor who needed a plaza like that and that he would find him. Sure enough, he did, and he made a decent commission for the company and himself in the process. If you look closely at his career, you will see scores of examples that prove persistence wins the day; persistence is the name of the game.

At another point, Charles came across an Armenian developer who had a couple of plazas with vacancies. In order to maintain a dialogue with the developer, Charles offered to fill those spaces. The developer was not interested in selling, and Charles was not interested in getting the tenants. His aim was to get the developer to sell the plazas and make himself a decent commission. About two years of dialogue paid off when we ended up selling two of his projects. Charles kept in touch with the developer and did even more business with him in subsequent years.

Another person who comes to mind is a young gentleman who spent hours and hours putting leases together for developers only to meet with one failure after another. It seemed that he would never make it, but a few years later, he was able to put the sites and tenants together to develop a few plazas. Today, he is rich, has a few properties of his own, and of course, a huge cash flow.

He did not have an MBA degree or anything like that, and he didn't need one, because he understood the importance of persistence.

Another friend who became very successful in the medical laboratory business is someone I also mentioned earlier: Gora Aditya. He started with a couple of people in a lab in the basement of a building and developed that small business into an empire employing over six hundred people at the height of his career. The man would just not give up, and it wasn't a degree that made the difference—it was his persistence. When it comes to pursuing a goal and following up on a routine basis, you won't find anyone better than Gora.

It is true that highly educated people don't necessarily make money. Rather, it's the persistent sons of bitches who do! I have offered some very convincing examples, but I could provide scores more. The key is not to give up.

Here's an example from my life.

I came to understand that highway billboards advertising products and services were good business and that many outdoor ad companies paid big money for them. I worked hard to get approval to put a sign on a small building with great exposure on Highway 401 but kept being rejected by the city or the Ministry of Transport. I was never discouraged, however. After three years of work, I the sign was approved. It rented for $135,000 annually when it was ready to go, and it is still being rented today.

There is no replacement for hard work. Being smart helps, but it does not take the place of hard work and perseverance. A formal education provides guidelines for people, but it does not teach them to be persistent in whatever they do. The value of persistence is something my father understood, and he always stressed the importance of being practical and listening to one's inner voice.

# EXPERIENCE IS USEFUL, BUT VISION IS THE KEY

There is simply no substitute for experience. No amount of theory or reading will compensate for the lack of it. Education in any field helps, of course, because it can guide you in the right direction. It is, however, experience that helps you make the right decisions. It is also important that you have a vision.

There are many examples illustrating how experience was key to the success of individuals who had a vision and the experience to make their dreams a reality.

Did you know that Henry Ford was not very well-educated? He did, however, spend a lot of time developing his inventions and learning from experience, and in the end, he created the first commercially successful automobile.

Did you know that Warren Buffett, the world's second richest man, was not rich to start with? He is a completely self-made man, and his success has never gone to his head.

Did you know that some of Toronto's billionaires started out as plumbers and bricklayers? They also had a limited education, but it was experience and hard work that got them to where they are today.

Did you know that an Italian lawyer, another multimillionaire, started out as an ordinary real estate lawyer who kept forming small partnerships with a few of his clients and became rich? Now, his sons are very reputable home builders.

I attribute my success to understanding the importance of vision relative to my success.

My community is growing due to immigration and the growth of families, and some years ago it was felt that we needed a cultural centre and a place of worship. The process was long, but I was determined, and I had a vision. Eventually, we succeeded in acquiring five acres of land near Major Mackenzie Drive and Woodbine Avenue in Markham. I was the chairman of the building committee, and I was able to achieve that dream. Hundreds of people and seniors now use the centre. Without a vision, the dream would have never been realized.

Remember: if you let yourself think "this is it," then it will be the end of the story. The day you feel satisfied with everything, progress stops. You must always have a vision; it's something almost everyone can achieve.

# 14
## PERFECT BARGAINS DO NOT EXIST

There is no such thing as the perfect bargain. It is rare to be lucky enough to end up with a real bargain in real estate or on the stock market. You will most likely have to settle for something within a range.

When buyers get into a project, they usually end up paying more than they intended. However, as long as the overpayment is within a reasonable limit, as long as it is not excessive, it is good business. You are not buying a project to make a little bit of money over the short term—you are buying it because you want to make a lot of money over the long haul.

Many great deals are lost, either by buyers or sellers, because of the last $5,000 to $50,000. In the grand scheme of things, the amount in dispute may not be more than one or two percent of the total project. There are always decisions we regret because we have let a good deal go for the sake of a few thousand dollars. This is why my advice to buyers and sellers is not to look at the last penny but to go on with life and settle for a bit more or a bit less. There is rarely a situation in which you will end up with the exact number you had in mind.

I have overpaid a bit on the various properties I acquired many a time, but in the long run, I have never regretted doing so. For example, everyone thought I had overpaid for a building on Forest Manor when I acquired it for $100,000 per suite. Five years later, the building was worth pretty close to $200,000 per suite, but even then it did not make sense to sell it as the operating income kept going up and up.

My advice is not to look for a perfect bargain. Don't lose valuable time when, ultimately, it won't matter if you end up paying a bit more or getting a bit less.

# SOME INTERESTING SITUATIONS

As I maintain links with India, my birthplace, I have encountered some interesting situations that I might not have elsewhere.

When someone wants to start a business in India, it is virtually impossible to find a property to rent, especially in big cities like Bombay (now Mumbai) or New Delhi. For that reason, many business people end up purchasing property. For one reason or another, some of these businesses do not succeed. For example, if the owners do not quite understand the law of supply and demand, they might take on a losing proposition. Over the years, I have, however, seen real estate become a savior in a place like Bombay. Values generally end up going so high that the owners can cover the losses incurred by the business and may even make some money when they close it.

A few years ago, some friends of mine put healthy deposits down on apartments to be built in a desirable neighbourhood in Bombay. The builder constructed the suites, but he took a real gamble by adding floors, even though zoning bylaws did not allow such density. Although the apartments were completed, the city denied the builder occupancy permits. In the end, the builder was required to demolish the apartments.

My friends really wanted those apartments, and they got them because even though their apartments had been demolished, they still had air rights—allowing increased density when financially feasible—which have value. My friends could have sold the rights to the builder to make some money, but they were wise, and they were rewarded for their decision. The builder pursued the matter, and the city eventually granted permission to add the apartments. And guess what? The Bombay market was so buoyant that in the interim, values went up, and my friends ended up making a fortune.

Rent control was established in Bombay in the early 1940s. Tenancy law was such that landlords could never ask tenants to vacate apartments nor were landlords allowed to raise the rent. As well, tenants were allowed to pass their tenancies on to their children and future generations thereafter. If tenants wanted to leave, they requested money from prospective tenants, however, the transfer required the landlord's permission. Consequently, the deal always involved three parties: the existing and future tenants and the landlord/owner. Because these tenancies had value, it became the norm for the tenants to get about two-thirds of the money and the landlord to get one-third each time a place changed hands. In better areas of the city, "key money" could amount to millions of dollars.

As land is in short supply, it is quite common to get older properties into "redevelopment", in which case a prospective builder provides alternative accommodation for existing tenants, gives them space in the new building, and sometimes offers them either a larger space or a sum of money. In many cases, negotiations take years because seventy percent of the tenants have to agree. Thus, tenants end up better off.

In many cases, purchasing a condominium apartment and keeping it locked up for the next few years was a paying proposition. Invariably, the market went up and the owner made a lot of money that could then be invested in something else.

# REAL ESTATE IS ABOUT ADDING VALUE 16

The whole game of real estate is about adding value over time so you make a profit. Value can be added in many different ways, so it is best if I give you some concrete examples to make it easier to understand how things work.

A few years back, we purchased some property on Midland Avenue south of Eglinton—two buildings with one hundred and seventy-four apartments in dire condition. The owners had not been interested in putting money into the buildings because they never believed in the project— they simply didn't have a vision. The purchase price was around $54,000 per suite. We decided to fix all of the brickwork, repair the concrete, replace the railings and windows, modernize the elevators, replace the old toilets with ones that saved water, put down new carpet, paint, add new roofs, a new parking lot and driveway, and get the tenancies in order. The bottom-line improved because we started to collect very good rent and also because we reduced many expenses. In about three years, we were able to resell the buildings for over $87,000 per suite, making a very handsome profit.

One building we are very proud of is 100 Pembroke Street, located in the Gerrard and Jarvis area. This building was bought with three partners, including myself, with only $300,000 down and a purchase price of $1,035,000. Of the ninety-seven small apartments, ninety-two were bachelors, each about two-hundred square feet, and the remaining five were one-bedrooms. The building was foreclosed on by the Canada Mortgage and Housing Corporation (CMHC) and had been very badly managed. There were forty vacancies when we acquired it in 1995, and the rest of the tenants were either prostitutes or drug dealers. It took us about two years to get the urgent repairs done and improve the tenancy. At the end of that period, each of the partners took home $60,000 on an investment of $100,000. However, in 2002, the building required improvements that cost a substantial sum of money, and my partners were not keen on investing additional funds. As a result, I bought them out, paying each of them $1 million for their investment of $100,000.

After I had assumed full ownership, I continued to add value to the property by investing in some worthwhile improvements. The balconies were in very bad shape, and the sliding doors had to be replaced. I had the crazy idea of enclosing the balconies, which took almost two years to get the project approved by the city. Most of the small bachelors got thirty to forty square feet of additional space, which added fifteen percent or more space to the living area, making them attractive for single adults in the downtown area. The apartments were also very affordable at $650 to $700 per month, which was a considerable increase over the rent we charged before, around $500. I also made the building energy efficient. As well, we replaced the roof and parking lot and restored the underground garage. We recently modernized the elevators. We have been offered $12 million for this project, but the cash flow prevents us from selling.

The eighty-five-year-old building of fifty-six units on Roehampton which I mentioned earlier, is another example that comes to mind. Before we purchased it, the building had seventeen owners and was badly managed. We acquired it for $3 million in 2006 and spent an average of $20,000 per apartment. When they turned over, we completely gutted and re-rented them for much more money. (We also created some interesting layouts.) As I said, the building sold for $8,225,000 in 2012, making a handsome profit for the investors.

Earlier, I also referred to a property at 24 Forest Manor Road in the Don Mills and Sheppard area, which we purchased toward the end of 2008. The hundred and twenty-eight units had been properly managed, but they required significant repairs. We replaced the roof, all of the windows, doors, and balcony railings, the parking lot, and did some landscaping. We also buried the swimming pool because it was only being used by a small fraction of the building's occupants, and this was how we created extra parking, which brought in additional revenue. The operating expenses of the swimming pool, in the order of about $20,000 per year, were eliminated.

The building was purchased for $100,000 per suite, and we have recently refused offers of $170,000 as the area is being redeveloped, and the building has the potential for additional coverage, meaning that we could bring money in without selling the building. Instead, we sold additional coverage to the owners of adjoining land. Such a move would allow greater density, as the coverage would be taken from our building and added to the development on the adjoining land.

You can also add value to land in the path of development. In many cases, one can, over time, get the zoning changed to subdivide the land or sell off pieces. The laws covering land can be tricky, and this is why one has to thoroughly study the area before venturing into this type of investment.

As I mentioned earlier, many years back, we assembled about two hundred and fifty acres of land in the Major Mackenzie and Woodbine area of Markham. These parcels were acquired for a total of $3.2 million and resold for about $21 million. We did not have to do much except wait for the huge profit.

Something important to understand is that you don't always need big money to add value. One of my associates rents a number of units at the Pembroke building, furnishes them, and re-rents them for a short term at a much higher rent to tourists, consultants, and the like. This strategy gets him a decent cash flow. Other people, whom I have known for many years, have done something similar with downtown condos they rent from the owners.

There are always opportunities to add value to a piece of real estate if you look closely enough. For example, you can add value by increasing the curb appeal. Someone looking to rent will always choose a building with attractive landscaping. The main lobby is another area that can be beautified and hallways that are carpeted and in good condition also help. Improving interiors will result in higher rentals. Renovating kitchens and bathrooms always pays in the long run.

# ANY TIME IS A GOOD TIME TO BUY

Over the course of my career, friends and clients frequently ask if it is a good time to buy. I tell them that almost any time is a good time to buy. You just have to make sure you are purchasing the right project.

My nephew owns a home in the Victoria Park and Finch area. When I started in real estate in 1972, I was sold a typical home there for around $27,000; it was a good time to buy. When my nephew bought his home about eight years ago, he paid $265,000; it was still a good time to buy. Now, homes in the area sell for $950,000—is it still a good time to buy? It certainly is.

Another example that comes to mind is the building on Roehampton Avenue that we have owned for some time. In the mid-1990s, some investors got together and purchased this building for about $1,450,000; that was a good time to buy. In 2005, we bought the very same building for $3,000,000; again, we thought it was the right time to buy. In 2012, after some renovations, we sold that building to an investor for $8,225,000. Very recently, the building was on the market, and I believe it sold for about $12,000,000. Would these people have regretted the purchase? Most likely not.

Timing is, of course, everything. Properties sell below replacement cost and sometimes above it. Charles Sachdev was stuck in the 1990s when he took more than $100,000 from his RRSP for a third mortgage on a multi-unit industrial property in Stoney Creek. There was one significant problem: there was a negative cash flow due to the number of tenants who had vacated the property. The members of the syndicate owning the property took a walk, and poor Charles had to take the property over. As I said in an earlier chapter, he was not, however, discouraged. He called his friend Murray, who specialized in renting industrial spaces in the area, and told him that he could be a partner in this venture for nothing, provided he looked after the renting. And Murray did. This property is now generating a very good cash flow, and both of them enjoy healthy monthly returns.

Over a period of ten years, we sold Fenworth Plaza in Hamilton five times to different buyers, and each time the sellers made money. Each time, it was a good time to buy, and no one lost any money.

During the 1990s, the economy was so bad that many buildings in Toronto were sold for $10 to $20 per square foot, which was lower than the rental value. Over time, the values rebounded, and buildings started to sell for much higher prices. Every time the property turned over, it seemed like it was a good time to buy.

It is important to remember that when there is an active market and prices go beyond your reach, you must not give up. You just have to look harder to find the right property, one to which you could add value.

# DON'T READ THE NEWS
# READ THE CLASSIFIEDS

Trust me: this is wise advice. I have gained so much from reading the classified ads in newspapers over the years. Of course, the number of print ads is declining, but you can still find similar ads on the Internet.

The news covers items over which most of us have little power. Although people can make a difference on a local level, it is extremely hard to change what goes on in the larger world because it is difficult to influence the decisions of world leaders. When you check out classified ads, however, you will end up dealing with "real" people, individuals with whom you can interact.

Reading the ads people place in newspapers and magazines can also give you some valuable ideas. Many specialty publications do not charge much for classified ads, thus providing a lot of opportunities for people to connect to buy, sell, or trade. With the advent of the Internet, many of these publications have become obsolete, but as I noted above, there are many websites to help people find each other in their place. One can still make deals.

Many years ago, when I was newly married, I had a really good idea from a classified ad. I used to import items from India. One very enterprising manufacturer fashioned tiny elephants from ivory waste left over after carving and putting them inside "lucky beans". Inspired, I rented a post box and started advertising these products as: "100 YEARS OF GOOD LUCK WITH 100 ELEPHANTS."

Bingo! My wife went to the mailbox every day to collect cheques after which she sent these lucky beans to our mail-order customers. Each one of them cost me just a few pennies, and the business provided a good side-income. We later introduced other small items—like hand-carved paper cutters—and mailed them out with the shipments to get repeat orders. I left the business when real estate began to take up more and more of my time, and so I did not follow up. However, I am convinced that it could have become a real moneymaker.

A few years back, I was in San Francisco, where my son lives. As I mentioned earlier, he had been trying to buy a place for himself, but the volatile market—in which you had to overbid by several hundreds of thousands of dollars to get what you wanted—made it was difficult. How could you possibly find a good deal in such a market?

I picked up the *San Francisco Chronicle* and real estate magazines, and I kept seeing ads stating "TICs for sale". As I mentioned earlier, I found out that TIC stands for "tenancy in common". The city allowed people to buy a bigger property—like a fourplex—and convert it to a TIC property. Each TIC could be then be acquired by an individual who would occupy one of the four units, similar to a condo. As well, you could enter into a real estate lottery in which the city allowed two hundred TICS to be converted into condominiums annually. I also discovered that some banks would finance TICs.

I quickly found a top-notch agent to buy a fourplex for my son. We overbid and purchased one in a very nice area for $1,650,000. One of the apartments—double the usual size—had been used by the owner who had rented out the rest. My son kept that one for himself. He was able to sell the other three for a gross amount of $1.3 million, out of which he paid commissions and legal fees. The value of the one he kept for himself was $1 million at the time. Even if we factor in a lot of expenses, the cost of his apartment was less than $500,000. He also had a garage that he rented out for $250 per month as he did not have a car. This deal was made possible because I read the classified ads.

At one point, I wanted to know what happened to the timeshares people bought while on holidays. It is common in many resorts for real estate agents to offer guests free breakfasts or discounted tours to entice them to give up a few hours of their time to attend a sales seminar. The strategy is often very successful because many people end up buying timeshares or other kinds of properties. When we were on vacation in Puerto Vallarta one time, I picked up a paper with ads for timeshares. As there is no real market for resale timeshares, I was able to pick up a timeshare for $11,500 that was being sold by my hotel for $38,500. Now, there are many websites offering thousands of timeshares at dirt-cheap prices.

With Google, Kijiji, Craigslist, and many other sites, the field is wide open. Just remember that when you respond to classified ads, you will deal with people one-on-one, and you will be able to persuade them to buy or sell. You gain very little by studying the news, but classified ads in print or on the Internet allow you to do some real wheeling and dealing.

# TOO BUSY MAKING A LIVING

A long time ago—probably about forty years, I read an article in *Reader's Digest* stating that "most of us do not make any money because we are too busy making a living." Having reflected on this observation, I am convinced it is true. I talk to many individuals who say they are simply so busy they do not have the time to think about—let alone start—a project that could make them a real fortune. The same holds true for most of us. There seems to be no opportunity for the kind of creative activities that might reap real financial rewards. It is, however, essential that you regularly take time off to reflect on what you have been doing, because you will probably come up with many excellent ideas as well as many new and interesting possibilities.

I have often come across individuals who work very hard for the companies that employ them. These individuals may work fourteen to sixteen hours a day, and sometimes seven days a week. They are busy making a decent living while making fortunes for the companies that employ them. I suggest they leave their jobs and do the same thing for themselves or take a leave of absence to explore opportunities, but no one seems to take that advice. They are just "too busy making a living", and consequently, they never make any real money.

I have been fortunate enough to take five or six weeks off almost every year, and I am always rejuvenated by that time, even when I am doing well. My trips to India, for example, are a reprieve and help me do new things. During my time away, I always come up with innovative ideas that my colleagues and I invariably use to our advantage. You should never let yourself become so busy that you have no time to consider fresh opportunities.

# 20
# LEARN HOW TO BORROW

It is important that you learn how to borrow, as well as to teach your children how to borrow and not to save. Saving money to make money does not make sense as the returns are pretty low. The point, of course, is not to borrow money simply to acquire goods, but rather to invest it and make more money. One of the best ways to grow your business is to borrow against the equity in your real estate—to leverage it.

As I have indicated, I came to Canada with practically nothing. Together, my friend and I had capital in the order of only $500 which we had borrowed from a friend in London, England. However, after a year or so, we had saved $1,000. Thanks to a credit union loan, we were able to purchase a ten-room house with a down payment of $6,000, and the rental income covered all of our expenses, including the mortgage. Due to circumstances beyond my control, I had to divest myself of my ownership after about three years but had we kept that house as an investment, it would have paid for itself. With the rise in real estate values, we could have borrowed against the equity and invested in even more income properties.

If you have purchased a home but do not have a family, you should consider renting an apartment for yourself and renting out your home. Not only will you have a healthy income, but you will also be able to obtain a line of credit from your bank that can be used for other investments. The following story illustrates this point.

On my advice, one of my nephews purchased a house with two basement apartments which he rented to use the monthly income to pay his mortgage. After a few years, the value went up, and I suggested he purchase an income property. Because he didn't have any liquid funds, I asked him to go to his banker to ask for the largest equity loan he could get against his house. He was approved for $140,000, and when I found him a seven-plex with steady tenants for $825,000, he and a friend were each able to make a down payment of $125,000. A few years later, when his mortgage came due for renewal, he was able to get a loan of $800,000. The income from the rentals was still enough to carry all their payments and expenses comfortably. He and his friend then bought another building, which had fourteen apartments. I wanted them to get more properties, but his partner got cold feet and did not go much further.

Someone else who learned how to borrow is Mark Knodell, whom I mentored for a number of years. (He would take me for breakfast at a nearby hotel so he could pick my brain.)

When I first met him, he had acquired two small buildings with about a dozen apartments. He had some capital and was able to buy a small building of twenty-eight apartments. The property required a lot of work, but he was able to get it into tip-top shape within the first couple of years. He was then able to buy another building on the same street that also required a lot of work. As I have explained, real estate investment is about adding value. Mark did just that, and he did extremely well—the man knows how to hustle. Five years later, he owns more than 300 apartments and so far has hardly sold any of his assets. He generally buys run-down properties and renovates them to improve the income. Then, he goes to the bank or another lending institution and borrows to make his next investment. His original equity of about $1 million is now more like $10 million. As you can see, real estate is not a complicated science. Mark was very successful, but there's no reason others can't also do well.

# 21
## INVEST IN YOUR OWN BACKYARD

If you live in a reasonably-sized city or town or are close to one, do not go elsewhere to invest. I have lived in Toronto for many years, and many of my friends live there as well. I can tell you that there is no place like this city in which to invest.

Many people see ads, do research, and go to sunny places like Florida or Mexico to invest in properties—condominium apartments in particularly. Because the down payments are so low and the monthly payments are less than the guaranteed income, these properties are very appealing. Unfortunately, within a few years, the guarantees run out, and the owners are left on their own. As you can imagine, there are many horror stories as a result.

Although there are many reasons these investments go sour, I am sure it's mostly the lack of personal attention. Many properties in Florida and other parts of the United States are sold at seminars and the people who attend them think the deals make sense because of what they see on paper when, in reality, they don't. It is important to remind yourself that the grass always looks greener on the other side and the mountains look gorgeous from a distance.

It always makes sense to own an income property in your neighbourhood or within a reasonable driving distance, because you can attend to any problems that arise or oversee the improvements you make to add value to your investment. It only makes sense to purchase property at a distance, say, in Florida, if you are willing to make a few trips there to study the market in the area you want to invest. If you do purchase a property, it is wise to get a local broker or property manager to help you out as you cannot be there all the time. Precautions like these allow you to take advantage of such investment opportunities and have a good return.

Always remember: invest in your own backyard.

# 22
# SALES SEMINARS

In previous chapters, I commented on the dangers of investing in properties in a market you do not know well. In connection with this, it is worthwhile to focus specifically on sales seminars.

There are all kinds of these seminars happening at any given time, but some of the most common are those in which the speakers advocate the purchase of properties in sunny areas like Florida. As noted in previous chapters, a lot of these investments look good on paper, but in practice, one seldom comes out ahead.

Having said that, I will also say that some seminars can be useful. For example, you can learn a lot from the apartment owners' conference held in Toronto and other major cities because you can network with other owners. You will also learn how to reduce your expenses or increase your income. Just remember to use discretion when you sign up for such seminars. Be careful, because practically all of the seminars are designed to get money out of you. For instance, when you go on vacation to, say, a resort, there are invariably breakfast or dinner seminars in which you are offered timeshares and other goodies, such as investments in condominiums, land, and the like. Keep in mind that nothing really comes out of their pockets when they give you a guarantee, but somehow or other, it is likely to come out of yours.

As I also explained in an earlier chapter, I used to visit one particular hotel complex to escape Canada's cold winter weather from time to time. Although I was interested in the timeshare, I was not willing to pay the list price of $38,500. Instead, I looked in the local newspaper for a timeshare resale. Because there is not much demand for them, I was able to pick one up that was marketed for $38,500 for $11,500 with about 38 years remaining—a great deal! I have been enjoying it ever since.

If you are interested in timeshares, simply go on the Internet. You will find hundreds if not thousands of people begging you to buy. You should be able to pick one up for twenty to thirty percent of the face value. You can even go to other places in the world, using RCI or a similar network.

The key point I want to make is that when you are tempted to buy something through a sales seminar, always check out the resale market before you do, because you are bound to find a better deal there. If you check the resale market, you find many impulse buyers who want to unload what they bought at one of those seminars, and they will likely be willing to make a good deal. It may not be quite as good as what is being offered at the sales seminar, but considering that you will pay thousands less, it will be good enough.

Whenever you read a newspaper or search the Internet, always keep an eye out for such a deal.

# 23
# ARE ALL TENANTS PROBLEMS?

When you talk to the average person about investing in a rental property, most of them will tell you, "Oh, tenants are nothing but a problem," without fail. This is a common fallacy that generally comes from people who have either tried to invest in a rental property or have never tried to make their money make money.

In my experience, at least ninety percent of all tenants are good people and tenants who will pay their rent and keep their apartments fairly clean at all times. Someone who purchases a property might have a problem with a couple of tenants who don't pay the rent or are habitually late in paying it, but these problems are not the norm. Don't forget that there are hundreds of landlords who own thousands upon thousands of rental apartments or commercial properties who carry on with their business because they get a much better return on their money than they would if they kept it in the bank. All of these landlords sleep well at night.

How is it that some landlords have bad tenants while others don't? Having a bad tenant once in a while is a fact of life, however, if you have a unit to rent, it is best to get an application from a potential tenant to get some necessary details. You can check the person's references, credit rating, previous landlords, present and previous employers, and so on. If you complete this task with good results and if you are friendly but firm, you will end up with a good tenant. People who are responsible, married individuals, immigrants, and students, and those with steady jobs generally make good tenants.

If you develop a solid relationship with the tenants in your building, and if you meet their needs, they will talk about your building to others. It does not take a lot to keep tenants happy. What is of the utmost importance is that you keep the building in good repair and maintain its curb appeal.

If you drive a car, you know that once in a while, no matter how careful you are, you are going to have an accident. If you sit at home and never take the vehicle out on the road, you are bound to have a good driving record, but then you don't go anywhere. If you want to make money from rental income, you will need to take a bit of risk, and yes, end up with a bad tenant once in a while.

# CATEGORIES OF REAL ESTATE

When you talk to people about real estate, you will generally find that most think of buying either a house or a condo to occupy themselves. Owning your own home is never a bad idea, but the property is not necessarily good as an investment. If you are single or newly married, it is possible the home you buy is much too large for your needs. As I have suggested elsewhere, in this case, you might consider purchasing the home and renting it out. If your requirements change, you can always re-occupy the home and take it from there. If values go up in the meantime, you can use your home as collateral for a good line of credit which will not cost you anything until you use it. You can then get money to invest in other properties by borrowing from this line of credit to combine the funds with other savings you may have accumulated. Although a home can increase in value over the years, most people need the home to live in. For that reason, you should always consider having another rental property on the side to fully benefit from your real estate investment.

I know of people who have owned their first home but who, when it came time to move, kept the property and used the equity they needed to buy their next home. They then rented out the first home, letting it appreciate over the years. I also know of people who now have three or four homes, all of which had been their private residence for a while. They kept their old homes when they moved and rented them out. This is an excellent way for many people to get on the investment bandwagon.

It is, however, important to understand that there are many varieties of real estate investments, each of which has its merits and pitfalls. As I have said, one can buy a house or two or condominium apartments and rent them out. This is a simple way of investing that does well over time for most people. One should, however, look at all the options before going forward with the investment.

As many people do not have large sums of money lying around, they should consider investing with a group. One can form a group by inviting a few friends, relatives, or co-workers to make a syndicate or partnership. Such a strategy will also allow various talents to come into play, and each of the partners can give input on an investment. One group of people, who got together in 1978 with my help, invested $5,000 to $10,000 each for five or ten percent interest in a land parcel north of Toronto. After about eight years of holding the property and making small monthly payments, those who had invested $10,000 ended up with $850,000, which is not a bad return.

The above is a perfect example of the benefits raw land investment could bring. Land in the path of future development can be a particularly good investment, as it requires hardly any work on the participants' part. There should, however, be a very good co-tenancy agreement so that everyone knows what will happen if a partner stops making payments or dies before the investment is sold. Many lawyers specialize in this type of agreement, and it is wise to go to one for advice.

It also makes a lot of sense to purchase a rental apartment building consisting of six or more apartments. With a group in place, one can buy into a building with fifty to one hundred apartments. At this level, however, it pays to have a superintendent on site, and you may also need to hire a property manager. Again, as the income goes up, so does the value, and one can refinance this investment as necessary.

Some people, either by themselves or in partnerships or joint ventures, have done very well with commercial shopping centres, which generally have strong tenants able to weather all kinds of economic conditions. Others have done well with multi-unit industrial tenants.

I have come across older apartment buildings that sit on large parcels of land. With cities allowing greater densities, these parcels become viable as excess land can be developed into other rentable units or condominiums. In municipalities like Niagara Falls, it is not too difficult to convert regular apartment buildings into condominiums. We purchased one—for which we paid an average of $54,000 per apartment—and after many renovations and upgrades, we sold the individual apartments at an average price of $150,000, which was still a great price for many people. Although it takes a lot of effort to complete the conversion process, it does pay in most cases.

Here is an example of a successful real estate investment.

Some thirty years ago, I sold some plazas to an investor who represented some people from Kenya. I was able to sell this individual a hundred-acre parcel in Markham with a lot of persuasion. The investors had to sell a couple of plazas when the economy went sour in the mid-1990s, and although they made a decent profit on one of them, they still took a bit of a loss. The one they are still holding, however, is giving them a very good return. I ran into this individual at a gathering and asked him how he was doing with the land. His answer was that they had refused $50 million for that particular property. Here is an important truth about the real estate business: one bad experience is no reason to shy away from investing.

One can increase the value of any real estate investment by increasing the bottom line. The idea is fairly simple: increase the income however you can and decrease the expenses. In many apartment buildings requiring capital improvements—like resurfacing balconies, changing railings or the roof, or restoring the underground garage— the authorities will allow you to pass on a certain amount, currently limited to three percent per year, to existing tenants. This approach increases the value of the investment, and for that reason, it is worth the exercise in most cases.

There are other ways to increase values: you can increase the density and develop the property or resell it at a higher price because of the increased density. There are people who have assembled a number of old houses by offering a higher price to the owners, putting deposits down on them, and later then amalgamated or bundled the properties so they could sell it to a developer as a single parcel. The value difference can put several million dollars into the pockets of an individual willing to take the trouble to put such properties together.

# INVESTMENT ANALYSIS

Investment analysis is not a very complicated process, as I explained earlier, one in which you do not need to engage consultants or accountants—a simple calculator and common sense are all you need.

For example, when we look at acquiring apartment buildings, we go through the data generally provided by real estate brokers and use that information to decide whether or not to go forward.

Let me define a few key terms for those of you who are not very familiar with real estate investment and offer some advice.

*Cap rates* generally give you an idea as to pricing. If you have cash available for investment and are looking to get, say, a five percent return, you would look for an investment sold at a five cap. The value of a building with an operating income of $100,000 would thus be $2 million if acquired at a five cap. However, the cap rate is just one factor you need to look at. If the building has a lot of upsides, you might decide to settle for a lower cap rate. Do not simply look at the cap rate and nothing else.

*Income multipliers* are another thing to consider. A building sold at a five multiplier—meaning five times the gross revenue—might not have a good cap rate, but it could still represent good real estate value. Some years ago, we acquired a couple of buildings on Midland Avenue in poor condition. The price, however, was five times the gross revenue while the cap rate was barely six, and they required many capital upgrades. It turned out to be a very good investment because the operating income increased tremendously once the capital improvements were made, and we were able to earn higher rents as a result.

The *unit price*—or *price per door*—is something many investors look at closely. In the case of the Midland buildings, the unit price was only $54,000 because the units were run-down, and the price was equal to a five multiplier. It was very good real estate value.

In the case of shopping plazas, quite often investors look at the price per square foot. In the mid-1990s, many buildings sold at $20 to $30 per square foot, which was far below the replacement value. However, due to vacancies and low rent, they hardly made any sense from an income perspective. With the upturn, the values improved, and investors made some good money. A building on Lawrence Avenue in Scarborough was purchased by one of our investors for $18 per square foot, far below the replacement cost. After just three years, the owner sold the building at about $60 per square foot. Later, the building sold for about $150 per square foot.

*Expense ratios* are part of another approach used to evaluate investments. Generally speaking, most older apartment buildings have an expense ratio of fifty percent, which means the operating expenses are fifty percent of the gross revenue. The cap rate is arrived at by looking at the operating income. In the case of the Midland buildings, however, the operating expenses were about sixty-five percent of the gross revenue. This ratio meant there was a lot of room to reduce expenses and create a higher operating income, resulting in a better cap rate and higher real estate value.

When you are about to acquire an apartment building or shopping plaza, it is important to go through the leases, tenant files, expense files, and other materials. The leases will give you an idea as to how steady the tenants are and the rent they are paying. Steady tenants do not always make a lot of sense because rent cannot be increased by improving the units; some turnover is healthy. Going through tenant files is extremely important because it gives you an idea of the type of tenants and problems the building may have. Tenant complaints tell you a lot about what you might end up with once you close the deal. If there are plumbing problems, you will know. Similarly, heating problems will tell you the status of the equipment.

One should be cognizant of capital expenditures. You need to know the amount of the funds needed to get the building up to par. Capital expenditures generally pay off in the long run, since the building becomes more desirable. Curb appeal is also important as it attracts tenants who want to rent in a good-looking building.

You also need to look at the average rent. Some years ago, as I mentioned, we acquired a very rundown building in the Yonge and Eglinton area that provided an average income of about $685 per month per apartment. They were small units, however, with all of the available conveniences, the rent was far too low for the area. A few years later, when the building was resold at a much higher price, the average rent went up to $850 per month, and it had the potential to go up even further.

The superintendent of the building makes a huge difference. A super can make or break the building and is a very important asset that needs attention. If you can keep a good super or husband-and-wife team, you will do well with your investment. Your supers are your twenty-four-hour watch, and they can add dollars to your investment.

When you look at an investment, you need to pay attention to income and expenses. If the income is lower, that is, if average rents are low for the area, it is an upside that will come in handy. If expenses are high, you know to cut them to improve the bottom-line. There are many buildings with old, thirteen-litre toilets which use a lot of water. These days, you can replace them with three-litre toilets. Also, newer showerheads will save a lot of water. Any savings on expenses will put more money in your pocket.

Many older buildings sit on large pieces of land. Given the increase in population and changes in zoning bylaws, it is sometimes possible to sever parts of the property to sell them off, thus reducing the cost base and improving the overall return. Some older buildings have many storage, locker, and empty spaces that could be converted into rentable apartments. We did this kind of conversion on a project on Morningside Avenue, adding fourteen apartments to the existing two hundred.

As I noted earlier, I developed the Rule of Ninety Percent from this experience. Before you make a purchase, you need to do an analysis of the real estate investment using various methods. When that has been done, you may still not be one hundred percent convinced about—or satisfied with—the proposition. At that time, it is good to ask yourself if you are ninety percent satisfied. In other words, if, after looking at everything, you are almost sure that a certain investment is good for you, then you should go ahead with it. Settle for ninety percent and leave the remaining ten percent to luck or risk. You need to take that much risk in life in order to get anywhere. There are no money-back guarantees in this business. When everything is said and done, your gut feeling is a good guide. Just go ahead—most of the time you will find yourself on the right side.

# SPECIAL-PURPOSE HOUSING

There are areas of real estate that cater to special purposes which can present good opportunities for extraordinary returns.

Student housing is one such area. It can be located near universities, colleges, or technical schools. Many students come from different parts of the country or from different parts of the world, for that matter, in need of housing within walking distance of educational facilities or a short bus or bike ride away. Parents want to see their children living in a good environment, and when they are spending tens of thousands of dollars on their child's education, it is likely they will not mind paying a little extra for housing.

Many purpose-built or converted projects cater to student housing. In general, apartments are divided into three or four bedrooms with shared living rooms and kitchens. As an owner, one can make a very decent income. One can also provide additional services like house-cleaning that parents really appreciate. They generally don't mind paying a bit more to ensure their children will be living in a clean environment. The building can also have video and game rooms, exercise facilities, and other services the residents can use.

One broker I know very well, Derek Lobo of Rock Advisors, has done extensive research in this area and is able to advise clients as to what to look for and how to develop such student housing. We have a building in Toronto located within walking distance of Ryerson University, and it always remains full of students.

One way to improve the income from a property is to convert it to a rooming house. Many large homes can be converted into rooms with facilities, such as stovetops and showers, and then rented to individuals to bring in a better revenue. Many people preferring to be closer to the downtown area to be nearer their place of work might also prefer to live in one of these rooming houses.

Furnished apartments always seem to be in demand. It is not unusual to find people coming to Toronto for short-term work as consultants, exhibitors, or to make sales. These people will pay above-average rent as they do not want to set up a household for that short period of time. In one of our buildings, an individual can rent a number of units from us and re-rent them at an above-average rate, making additional revenue by furnishing them. His investment is limited to the cost of furniture, which is minimal but decent, and he makes a very good living. I also know another individual who rents condos from other investors in luxury buildings, providing the renters with very good furniture. He rents these condos at a much higher rate and makes a decent living at it.

Assisted living is another area able to provide an opportunity to maximize the return on an investment. There are many seniors who are independent but who could use services like grocery shopping and cleaning among others. Such services can even be provided in an existing rental building, making rental attractive to residents while bringing in additional revenue.

Disabled people need to live in buildings that do not require the climbing of stairs. Living areas can also be modified with specially designed kitchens and bathrooms.

Again, such rental buildings are attractive to residents who would not mind paying a higher rent to ensure they have what they need.

Retirement homes are needed in almost every community. These homes provide a variety of apartments and dining facilities which many older people like. Residents also have the company of other people in their age cohort, and many activities can be scheduled that are geared to helping them, such as shopping outings or escorting them for appointments that can be provided.

# 27
# REAL ESTATE VS. THE STOCK MARKET

When we talk about returns, many individuals compare the returns on real estate to those on the stock market. However, investing in real estate presents its own pitfalls and opportunities, which is why the two should not be compared.

Many people find the stock market easier to understand and feel the liquidity the market provides makes it more worthwhile than real estate. Real estate cannot be traded like stocks because in real estate, one has to have a much longer view. As such, it does not provide the stock market's liquidity.

When shares of, say, Bell Canada are sold on the stock market, all of the shares are priced the same, but in real estate, no one investment is identical to the next. The investors in real estate make their decisions on an individual basis at any given time. They look at opportunities from very different perspectives than other investors. Similarly, a seller of real estate may have his or her own way of selling, and the pricing criteria could be entirely different.

One situation I encountered will make my point clear. Someone working for us, watching what we were doing, came across a small apartment building (twenty-two units) owned by an eighty-six-year-old individual who wanted to sell. When the employee told me she could purchase the building for $900,000, I found it hard to believe. The property sold for hundreds of thousands of dollars below its market price, irrespective of its condition. (It is hard to comprehend why the seller accepted such a low price.) A few years later, after an investment of about $300,000, the building sold for a net profit of over $1 million. Again, a situation like this cannot occur in the stock market as all stocks are traded on a stock exchange. There are no special circumstances of which you can take advantage.

Real estate investments present you with opportunities to add value; stock market investments do not. You cannot buy shares of Bell Canada and do anything to add value on your own. In real estate, however, you can purchase an old house and add value by renovating it.

Although stocks can be margined, they are not as good as real estate where you can make an investment, improve cash flow, and practically pull out of the entire investment to invest in other properties. As well, you can create demand for rentals by providing services needed in the area. You cannot do that if you own shares.

Many individuals have abilities that can help improve the bottom line on real estate investments. For example, in the 1990s, when many investments failed, a colleague of ours ended up with a large industrial building with many tenants. He was able to get it without really investing any money or a down payment because the owners could not meet the payments on the existing financing. He knew somebody who was good with leasing and gave him half the share for his work, filling up the building. After some years, they collected a decent, monthly revenue as the building remained full. Such opportunities are not possible with stocks because one does not have much control over them, however, one has all the control with real estate.

Another difference between the stock market and real estate is that one needs to be vigilant with stocks and watch the market. In real estate, however, this is not the case as nothing changes overnight. One can take the time to work on the investment and improve it by getting good tenants, for instance. This is hardly a possibility in the stock market.

In conclusion, I can say that, yes, one can make money by investing in the stock market, however, your fate is not decided by you, but rather, by market conditions and economy or the people who have issued the shares. Real estate is different because your investment gives you the freedom to make decisions and add value.

# CONDO CONVERSIONS

Converting an existing rental building into a condominium building is a great way to add value to real estate. In most cases, it pays to make the change. Although the process is quite complicated and takes a fair amount of time, it is worth considering.

We have had very good experiences with condo conversions in the city of Niagara Falls. We acquired three good-sized rental buildings there and were able to get condo status. We catered to the end users—that is, the residents who wanted to own the apartment rather than rent it. There are not that many condominium buildings in that city, and so we had no difficulty marketing these buildings to the end users.

The perfect example of a successful condo conversion was our building at 4658 Drummond Road in Niagara Falls, which had a variety of rental units—seventy-eight of them—ranging in size from about 700 to 1,400 square feet. It was purchased for an average of $54,000 per unit and sold for an average of $150,000. It is was a three-storey, U-shaped building with a courtyard, located on about four acres of land. It is now mostly occupied by seniors.

In many outlying cities such as Niagara Falls, St. Catharines, and Hamilton, it is possible to convert existing rental buildings into condominiums. The condo status is governed by the vacancy rate in the area at any given time. Cities are not interested in destroying rental stock, and they only grant condominium status if there is more than enough rental supply. If the vacancy rate is five percent or greater, there is every hope of getting the conversion approved.

As rental buildings are generally sold based on the operating income, the price per unit is likely to be much lower than the price per unit in condominium buildings. All of our buildings in Niagara Falls were acquired for around $50,000 per unit. They were completely renovated, both inside and out, and sold to individual owners for about $150,000 per unit.

People who rent apartments pay the prevailing rent in the area. The values of rental buildings do not reflect the replacement costs, which are generally higher. However, people who want to own their own apartment will pay the market price. In these situations, they do not mind a higher price, as they will own something that will always have value; a rental apartment does not build equity for the renters.

There are also marketers who convert rental buildings into a condominium building and sell off individual units to investors. The tenants continue to live there, and nothing really changes for them. The people who sell individual units to investors do the management, and when possible, give dividends to the owners. For smaller investors who do not have the down payment required for larger projects, this is a great way to own real estate.

In Toronto, conversion to condominiums is difficult, however, the city permits conversions for buildings smaller than six units. We have converted five rental townhouses to individual street townhouses. A four-unit Victorian house was converted to condominium status in downtown Toronto and sold to owner-users. *The Globe and Mail* published an article about this project on July 13, 2012, as it really turned out well. In the article, the writer wrote the following:

> One man who believes that such discriminating home hunters do exist in the marketplace is Mac Champsee, president of Toronto based Rainbow Realty Ltd. and the developer (along with Sonal Champsee, his daughter) of an especially lovely, thoughtful condominium conversion at 103 Pembroke Street, west of Cabbagetown and just south of Allan Gardens.

After the owners got condo status, some churches that had lost their congregations were also converted into individual units for homeowners. Also, some obsolete industrial buildings were converted into lofts. Lofts have become very popular as they offer high ceilings and good locations in a city like Toronto. There is also great potential in converting these old industrial buildings, many of them over one hundred years old, into smaller, industrial units that can be sold to smaller users who get to own their units. Many of the buildings can be purchased for reasonable prices and sold at a good profit.

San Francisco is a good example of a city where older homes are being converted into four or five individually owned units. It is quite difficult to own a large house in that city as the prices are steep, and these conversions are a good way for individuals to own their residences.

In Toronto, there are many houses in Rosedale or Forest Hill that are too big for today's requirements. As families are much smaller, there are not as many people who want to own a 6,000-square-foot house—they'd rather own a 1,000-square-foot condo. Such condos could be very popular, as the area is extremely desirable for many individuals. Converting such houses into condos in these areas could prove worthwhile.

There are schools whose size exceeds the needs of the neighbourhoods, and these can also be converted to condominiums.

If you look around, there are opportunities everywhere.

# SYNDICATIONS AND JOINT VENTURES

Real estate investments can involve large sums of money, making it difficult for individuals to own multiple properties. It is also risky for an individual to own property, but owning a small part of a syndicate allows you to share the risk. Whether it involves a parcel of land, an apartment building, or a shopping plaza, a properly run syndicate is a good way to own.

We usually have anywhere from four to twelve individuals able to form a joint venture to purchase a variety of real estate properties. One of the individuals or a management company can run the day-to-day affairs of the syndicate, a responsibility that periodically involves the collection or distribution of funds. We have had very good experiences in syndications and joint ventures and have done hundreds of them over the years. They worked out very well for most people in general. We did, however, suffer some losses in the 1990s when the market dropped sharply, but because the investment was divided among many individuals, most people survived just fine.

A properly drafted joint venture agreement is needed to cover every situation that might arise in detail. One that is well-drafted states the names of all the co-tenants, together with the individual interests. It appoints a management committee—generally of two or three individuals—whose members make the day-to-day decisions and who are required to call meetings as and when major decisions must be made. The agreement also sets out what happens in certain situations, for example, compensation paid to members who default or want to get out of the syndicate. It also specifies steps to be taken in case of a member's death. As well, there are provisions for the transfer of individual interests to spouses, children, or a corporation controlled by a member. Should an individual receive an offer to purchase his or her share, the interest is generally offered to the remaining members of the syndicate first. Only when they declare they are not interested in such an acquisition does it become available for sale to outsiders. Such outsiders then have to sign the joint venture agreement and follow all of the rules and regulations.

Not everyone is cut out to be part of a syndicate. Many people do not want to be governed by the decision of the majority. For those individuals, such an arrangement is not a wise choice. If you would, however, like to benefit from the advantage of larger sums of money, this is the way to go. It is best to enter into such a venture with people who you know to some degree, rather than total strangers. It is not a very difficult process, because there are many individuals who do not have large sums of money to invest on their own. Yes, profits are divided, but so are the risks. The risks get shared by the group, and the impact on you is less, should problems arise.

# BELIEVE IN YOUR PRODUCT

Over the years that I have been in business, I have come across many real estate sales professionals, investment advisors, and consultants who guide clients interested in investing in real estate. They do all kinds of analyses and projections to help their clients make investments and benefit from their ownership.

I have, however, seldom seen any one of these professionals apply what they preach when it comes to their own dealings. They help their clients and see many of them get rich and multiply their assets, but rarely do I see them investing in real estate themselves, although many of them own cottages in addition to their homes. This is rather silly, as people with firsthand knowledge should think about their own interests while helping their clients to invest their funds. I have helped many clients, and at the same time, made investments on my own. In the long run, I see the investments I did on my own far surpassed the commission income I derived from the sales of similar investments to clients.

There are, of course, exceptions. One of them whom I know very well. owned about six-hundred and fifty apartment units.

It is about time that sales professionals believe in their own product. While you are proposing projects for your clients to invest in, you should also think about yourself. This way, you can set an example for yourself as well as the people you deal with. Your clients will also get other prospective clients excited about investing with you when you prove to them what you have been able do with your own funds. So get sold on your own projects, as they will pay you in the long run.

Mac Champsee

# THE IMPORTANCE OF TRUST

If you are involved in the business of real estate sales involving large sums of money, your clients need to believe in you. You must prove to them that you are trustworthy before they will invest their funds through you. You must sell yourself before you can sell the property. This point is extremely important. Even if everything about a property makes sense, a client's trust in you is a major thing. A client has to trust your words before he or she will invest.

How do you get yourself to that level? You must get yourself known to people with money.

This is a long process involving joining groups like ratepayers associations, church groups, and other community organizations. You also need to educate yourself by attending various seminars and city meetings, learning the ropes, the intricacies of zoning and bylaws, and everything that goes with it. You need to know the rentals prevailing in a given area, the average income of the neighbourhood, and the development potential, all of which might affect values.

You need to keep going without stopping. Your progress ends the day you feel satisfied with your life. When you give a promise to your clients, you need to make sure that you can follow through. Do not make promises you cannot keep.

Positive thinking is very important. As well, you must be able to maintain your equilibrium because you just cannot afford to lose your temper. It is said that a good salesperson is the one who listens, not one who talks. It is important that you listen to your clients and others, as what you hear will guide you to make the right decisions.

37524320R00070

Made in the USA
Lexington, KY
27 April 2019